W9-BTN-856

Saving the Farm

A Journey Through Time, Place, and Redemption

To Lucy
thanks for helping
to keep the past
alive!

1/12/13

Saving the Farm

A Journey Through Time, Place, and Redemption

James T. Powers

HOMEBOUND
PUBLICATIONS
Independent Publisher of Contemplative Titles

PUBLISHED BY HOMEBOUND PUBLICATIONS

Copyright © 2013 by James T. Powers
All Rights Reserved

All Rights Reserved. Without limiting the rights under copyright reserved above, no part of this publication may be reproduced, stored in or introduced into a retrieval system or transmitted in any means (electronic, mechanical, photocopying, recording or otherwise) without the prior written permission of both the copyright owner and publisher except for brief quotations embodied in critical articles and reviews.

An effort has been made to trace the ownership of all copyrighted material contained in this book, to request permission where necessary, and to use that material in accordance with the terms of fair use. Errors will be corrected upon notifying the publisher.

The Power of Now Copyright © 1997 by Eckhart Tolle. Reprinted with permission of New World Library, Novato, CA. www.newworldlibrary.com.

"Old Barns and Men" © 1996 by Sam A Jackson. Reprinted with permission of the author.

For bulk ordering information or permissions write:
Homebound Publications, PO Box 1442
Pawcatuck, Connecticut 06379 United States of America

VISIT OUR WEBSITE WWW.HOMEBOUNDPUBLICATIONS.COM

THIS TITLE IS ALSO AVAILABLE IN EBOOK.

FIRST EDITION
ISBN: 978-1-938846-06-9 (pbk)

BOOK DESIGN

Cover Image: © 2010 James T. Powers
Cover and Interior Design: Leslie M. Browning

Library of Congress Cataloging-in-Publication Data

Powers, James T., 1953-
    Saving the farm : a journey through time, place and redemption / James T. Powers. —First edition.
        pages cm
    Includes bibliographical references.
    ISBN 978-1-938846-06-9 (pbk.)
    1. Dudley Farm Museum (Guilford, Conn.) 2. Dudley family. I. Title.
    S548.5.C8P69 2013
    636.009746'7—dc23

                                                            2012048166

For Rita, the light of my life.

CONTENTS

Introduction

You know the feeling—that gentle tug of a place that draws you to it. You may not at first even be aware of it or the pull might be instantaneous. What draws you there? Why? Is it a sight, smell, or a memory from your past that is jarred? The connection you feel is undeniable as you look around and drink it all in. You feel comfortable there, like the familiarity of home. For each of us what attracts us is a matter of personal experience, preference and choice. But, the message is clear—this place is somehow part of us; it's a whisper of who we were, are, or would like to be that draws us in and gives us pause.

For each of us the experience is a bit different. It might be the solitude and solace of a place that attracts us or the sense of community and the warmth of friendship. For others it might be a sense of familiarity. It may be the special beauty of a place or the humbling feeling that we are in the midst of something somehow greater than ourselves that gives us a sense of belonging. Maybe it's the simple recognition that where you are represents a different time and place, a window into another world gone forever.

What follows is a series of personal reflections, observations, history, and essays about just such a place. Along with a group of others, I began a journey of sorts in 1991 to help preserve and create a place that has drawn hundreds to it and in the process has given us each that sense of connection. It's a place of solitude, community, and beauty as well as an island of the past in a rushing tide of change—a place to pause, reflect, and experience. It is of all things—a farm.

Located on ten acres of woods and meadows at the intersection of two busy state roads, the Dudley Farm at first glance looks like many other surviving farms from the 19th century throughout New England. But, with a second look, it becomes obvious there's a difference. Sitting on a slight hill above the road, with its picket fence and stone walls, the farm calls the passer-by. The regal house and weathered barn have a bearing of permanence and strength as they cling to the land like the Yankee farmers who built them. The meadows and woods climb gently beyond and with the buildings evoke a different time. They draw you in—you look and you're hooked.

But that's only part of the story of the farm. It's also about the Dudley family who for six generations, worked the soil and did their best to survive for over 200 years. Nothing historic happened on the farm nor did any person of importance live there. But, day in and day out they worked, loved, laughed and cried; their farm is a reflection of who they were. Through it we can gain a glimpse into their world; to touch, see and feel the past.

This is also the tale of how the Dudley Farm was saved to become a museum dedicated to the preservation and representation of our rural past. By itself, that story may not be of any great importance, but to the small group that took on the task and the hundreds who have supported their effort to preserve the farm it was. At a time when farms are all but gone in Connecticut, the struggle to save the farm for future generations took on a crusade like quality. For those who struggled to bring the farm to life and the hundreds who visit each year, the Dudley Farm is a special place that tugs at the essence of who we are and were.

Although what happened at the Dudley Farm is unique to Guilford and the surrounding towns in Connecticut, it strongly speaks to issues of development and growth on a regional and national level. During the late 20th century, Guilford, like so many other communities nationwide experienced unprecedented levels of development and sprawl that forever transformed the very fabric of the community and threatened to destroy much of the unique cultural and historical heritage that had evolved there over 300 years. That transformation and the toll it was taking on the small and once insular community of North Guilford, the home of the Dudley's and their neighbors since the first decades of the 18th century, was the prime motivating factor in the determined effort to save the farm. When faced with the seemingly unending grind of residential and commercial development that characterized the era, a lament repeated in neighborhoods across Connecticut, New England, and the nation could be heard—is this what we want? As each farm disappeared and each woodland succumbed to the sprawling drive of relentless growth, the Dudley's farm became a symbolic connection to an agricultural and cultural heritage that was vanishing forever. It was there that a stand was made and thus a lesson for any community that might face the same crisis wrought by the sprawl of modernity. Can the heritage and history that has made us who we are be preserved for future generations or will it be lost forever in the name of progress?

Sure, there are many other historical properties and museums, Connecticut and New England are full of them. The small town of Guilford has five others. Laudably, each preserves an important slice of history from the 17th Century to the early 19th that allows us to peak into the past. Yet, the Dudley Farm is somehow different because it is a story unique in the context of time and place. What has happened there in the years since 1991 is quite remarkable—a story of a community of different people working together to save a place they all became connected to for the present and future generations. They made a stand, they saved the farm and with that a connection to the past.

Chapter One
Waving to David

Consider the past and you shall know the future.
— CHINESE PROVERB

I can still vividly recall the first time I noticed the Dudley Farm, a sight that has been with me since and it typified my image of the farm for most of the next ten years. I was returning home from an interview for a job teaching history at Guilford High School in August of 1983. As I passed through the intersection of Ct. Routes 80 and 77 heading north I was absorbed in how the interview had gone and hoping I would soon be making this drive on a regular basis. Suddenly to my right I saw what could only be described as a vision from the past. There standing by the porch of his stately but weathered home was a man dressed in old blue denim overalls, a long sleeved shirt, and a straw hat. Together with the white clapboarded house, the faded barn, and the rustic nature of the grounds, the scene was straight out of the 19th century, 1883 to be exact. I slowed my car to a crawl to capture the image in my mind when suddenly I did something that surprised me—I waved. I know the man saw me, but he did not react, he just went about his business and so did I.

That's the way it was for the next eight years as twice a day I would drive past the farm on my way to and from work. It was always a seasonal postcard from Currier and Ives; the farm house on the slight rise above the road, its white shuttered facade fading and a bit peeled, the weathered gray barn majestically set to the right and the sweeping hill with meadow and woods behind. The summer leaves turned the colors of autumn, the barren starkness of winter softened by snow, then the lush greens of spring. As the months and years passed the view became my haven from the 20th century—a vision of the past that would often reminded me of why I loved and taught history to begin with.

Most days the gentleman in overalls did not appear but his presence was often betrayed by the lone light in the rear of the house during the morning commute or by other hints of his activities. Plastic bags were stuffed with leaves and lined up against the foundation in winter, bundles of sticks collected for kindling, and wisps of smoke that gently rose from the back chimney. On occasion the great center bay doors of the barn were left open revealing his old pick-up waiting patiently for its next mission, the only sign of the present to intrude on the past. Every once in a while I'd see him, walking about his farm, coming from the barn, or fussing near the house. His appearance seemed to never change—overalls, but his hat changed seasonally; a narrow brimmed slouch hat in the spring and fall, straw in the summer, and a red and black checkered plaid in the winter. His tall thin build and the ease of his movements betrayed his lineage—a Yankee farmer from another time, just like his farm.

When the farmer was in view, I often slowed down fascinated by my peak at the past. If he noticed me I'd wave but he never waved back. I often told myself if he did return my gesture, I'd stop for a chat. As the months went by my list of questions grew as did the anticipated answers about his farm, life, family, and the story of the place he had always known as home. But, he never waved and I never stopped. No one at work knew much about the gentle man and his farm but over the years some of the kids knew him as the "old farmer". To the few I encountered who actually knew him or of him, he was David Dudley, a gentle, quiet, and private man who kept to himself and lived alone in the big farm house.

Change was coming to Guilford. By the late 1980's the town had exploded in a frenzy of suburban development and was transformed forever as what were left of the old farms that had characterized it's past 350 years disappeared, the woods became neighborhoods, and the schools filled to bursting with eager faces. Yet there it was David's farm, a developers dream. I lamented the farm's probable future and, like so many others I would find out later, hoped its demise could somehow be prevented. Maybe, just maybe, the house, barn, and land could be saved from being carved up by the inevitable asphalt of progress.

Then one day it happened—though exactly when I cannot recall. I was running late and in a hurry to get home one afternoon when I saw Mr. Dudley. Almost instinctively I slowed down and waved as I passed when to my surprise a lanky arm waved back. After all those years he had waved! In my excitement I almost forgot that I was late for picking up my kids as I all but slammed on my breaks to go back and introduce myself. But I couldn't. I vowed to pull in the drive and up to the old barn the very next time I saw him outside and eagerly hoped it would be soon. But that time never came. At first things seemed as always around the farm as the days turned to weeks but he never appeared.

Ominously, the character of the farm began to change as suddenly there seemed no sign of Mr. Dudley's presence and the buildings and grounds became forlorn. Soon it became clear I had lost my chance to speak to him and his farm was now in danger. As I passed each day I knew that the bulldozers of change would be perched, ready to strike.

That's the way it seemed to be, I would witness the farm's inevitable doom and with it another piece of the past, gone forever. But, the farm remained, clearly unoccupied and slumbering in its dignity. Then one day in late 1991, an odd thing happened. My dependable little pickup truck began to buck and all but stalled as I passed the farm. Annoyed, I shrugged it off as bad gas and thought nothing more of it. About a week later it happened again at the very same spot, right in front of the farm. I changed my gas filter and moved on—until it happened again. It was the only place in my travels it happened. Was it my gas filter or fate?

The history of David Dudley's family can be traced back to the founding of Guilford as a settlement in 1639. During the summer of that year three small ships sailed into the harbor at Quinnipiac (now New Haven, Ct.) having survived the perilous voyage across the Atlantic from England. Twenty seven year old William Dudley and his wife Jane must have gazed in nervous anticipation at the one year old settlement perched at the water's edge. They had come to what they and the others believed was an untamed wilderness as members of the Whitfield

Company, formed as part of an English Puritan migration determined to help establish a "new" England as a beacon of hope and example for the old.

Ten days into their journey while still at sea, the men of the Whitfield Company drew up and signed an agreement known as the Guilford Covenant. In it, they pledged to "... sit down and join ourselves together in one entire plantation and be helpful to each other in any common work according to every man's ability and as need shall require ..." [1]

Like the other signatories, William had given up his former life as a young man of property to help start a new society based upon Puritan teachings and values. Their pledge to one another in the Covenant epitomized the nature of the settlement and history of Guilford and later North Guilford of which some of William's descendants were to play an important part. Of the twenty five men who signed the Covenant, David Dudley could claim six as his ancestors.

William and the others had come to America as followers of the Rev. Henry Whitfield, a well-respected and influential Puritan minister, in an attempt to find a haven for their beliefs. Those beliefs had been at odds with the established Church of England since the 1620's over issues of church reform and practice. Questioning the church was tantamount to treason against the king, and many Puritans and their leaders were imprisoned, had property confiscated, or were in other ways persecuted. Between the years 1630 and 1640, over 40,000 Puritans came to New England as part of what became known as the Great Migration. They established communities in Massachusetts, Connecticut, Rhode Island, and New Hampshire which quickly became known as the New England Colonies. The settlement of Guilford was part of this great endeavor.

The leaders of the Whitfield Company wasted little time in acquiring land for their new settlement upon their arrival at Quinnipiac. They located a promising spot to the east of Quinnipiac called Menunkatuck by the native inhabitants who they met with and traded for the land. By September 1639, the new Puritan community of Menunkatuck Plantation had been established. During the first fragile decades of settlement, William and Jane Dudley raised four children; William, who was born during the voyage in 1639, Ruth, Deborah, and Joseph. It was through Joseph that David Dudley's family was descended.

William Dudley became a leader within the small community that clung to the shore of Long Island Sound on the southern coast of Connecticut and like their fellow settlements in the colony, slowly began to prosper. He was respected enough by the other planters in Guilford, which Menunkatuck had been renamed, to be chosen representative to the colonial legislature then called the General Court. By the time William died in 1674, the Dudley family, like the community he had helped to create, was well established in the new land.

Captain William Dudley, the grandson and namesake of the first William, became the first member of the family to actually live in what is now North Guilford the section of town in which the Dudley Farm is located. During the 17th century, the planters of Guilford, as the settlers were called, sought to open and occupy new land within the town boundaries. These expansions were called divisions and were controlled communal events designed to ensure each family received its proper share of lands to be opened. Individuals were not allowed to strike out on their own and establish land claims within the town's limits. Orderly settlement based upon established Puritan religious, social, and economic practices and beliefs were the guiding determinants. By 1692, the leaders of Guilford had decided that it was time for the land that was to become North Guilford be divided and parceled out to each male within the community.

This was the fourth time land in Guilford had been divided during the 17th century and like the others, the land for the Fourth Division was surveyed and allotted by a select committee of prominent townsmen. In dividing the land, the committee followed specific guidelines, among them that:

- Each male land holder receive one acre for every pound value they had been assessed for the holdings recorded in the 1690 Tax List.
- 18 acres were given for every male child under the age of 16.
- 10 acres were given for each woman and female child in the family.
- Land was made available to every "planter and proper inhabitant" who had lived in the town for at least five years.

The town also reserved certain sections of land bordering water sources as common land for the community.

Although the land was surveyed in 1692, actual lots were not assigned until 1705 and 1706. Each planter was asked to decide whether they wanted land in North Guilford or what is now the northern section of the neighboring town of Madison, to the east. They could also choose whether their share of the division should be apportioned together as a family group or in separate segments. As the new land holders began the arduous process of clearing, fencing, and working their land allotments, they traveled the eight to ten miles north from town on Monday and stayed together in small dwellings built for that purpose until Saturday when they would return to their homes in Guilford's village. It was because of this practice of living in the communal houses that the area received its early name of Cohabit.

This was the setting in which young William Dudley (1684-1761) and his wife Ruth moved to Cohabit as part of a general migration of Guilford families in 1712. It had been twenty years since the decision to allow settlement and six since the holders were actually permitted to work their new lands. Anticipation must have been high as the families trekked northward into what they saw as wilderness so recently made suitable for settlement. William's father Joseph Dudley (1643-1712) had died that year leaving William his lands in the Third and Fourth Divisions. It may have been his father's death that actually motivated William to move north to what were now substantial holdings in Cohabit.

Shortly after the move, the first of William and Ruth's ten children was born, a daughter named Submit. Of their ten children, five were to die during infancy or childhood including Submit and two infant boys both named William. Two other daughters, Lois and Sarah, died on the same day in October, 1743, victims of disease. Family tragedies and losses such as these were common during the 18th century as childhood disease and accidents took a high toll. The gravestones of these five children of William and Ruth can still be seen alongside those of their parents in the North Guilford Cemetery which William helped to establish and illustrate the price often paid by families struggling to survive in a world so different than our own.

By 1716, the settlers of Cohabit had become established enough to petition the town and the Connecticut General Court for the right to hire a minister for the winter months, eliminating the need to travel to Guilford proper for the day-long church services each Sunday. As the colony's legislature, the General Court was made up of representatives from each community and held decision making power for both secular and religious matters. Permission was granted to the settlers of Cohabit and by 1720, they were granted the right to raise taxes to establish and erect their own church. By 1725 the church had been built and a permanent minister hired. In their Puritan world, this marked for the settlers of what was now North Guilford, the fulfillment of the settlement process that had begun thirty three years earlier. Throughout that process, William Dudley had played a pivotal role.

Since the start of settlement in 1712, Dudley was looked to by his fellow settlers of North Guilford as a leader much as his father Joseph and grandfather William had been in Guilford. He was elected to the important position of captain of the North Guilford Militia by its members, an honor usually based upon a person's leadership skills and personal integrity. Captain William, as he became known for the rest of his life, also served the church society of North Guilford as one of its two deacons, a position second only to that of the minister in importance to the community.

A look at Guilford Land Records reveal that Captain Dudley from the onset in 1712 purchased and sold numerous tracts of land in North Guilford, Guilford, and surrounding communities, a practice he continued up until the time of his death in 1761. In an era when land was the true measure of wealth, the Captain became one of the most prosperous individuals in the community he had helped to create. Among the parcels he purchased was the one that his descendant David Dudley would call home. In his will, written just prior to his death in 1761, Dudley gave to his seventh child and third surviving son Jared (1727-1811), numerous tracts of land located throughout North Guilford and Guilford. Already a substantial land holder in his own right, Jared thus acquired land from his father that would become the Dudley Farm in the future. As William Dudley put down his quill, having written his will, he must have looked back on his life with satisfaction knowing he had contributed greatly to the establishment of a new and growing community and had preserved for his family, a legacy of land that he felt confidently would secure for them their place in the future.

Interlude Number One

(The following is an essay that appeared in the Dudley Farm Newsletter, Winter/Spring, 2004. In it I wrote of the Dudley Farm and its magical pull on those who visit).

A Sense of Place

Most of us have a special place, one we can escape to when the struggles of our day to day existence wear us down. It is a place we can go to slow down, take stock, and recharge ourselves before we go on to face the onslaught of daily life. This place of refuge is different for each of us—it can be your home, the kitchen, or a special chair. It might be a quiet spot in the woods, your garden, or the back deck. Above all else, it is a place of comfort that allows you to reconnect with your world, a place that is safe and somehow harmonious. You feel better for being there. It is there you have a sense of place.

For those who lived on the Dudley Farm one hundred years ago, a sense of place was probably much more extensive. Although they lived in a rapidly changing industrial world, their basic day to day life was much more attuned to the natural cycles of the day, the seasons, and nature. One hundred years ago, life on a farm followed natural rhythms in ways we would find surprising and their knowledge of and ability to respond to those rhythms now seems remarkable. When the Dudley's and their neighbors awoke each morning, the sounds, smells, and sights they experienced reflected that natural world around them. They knew their home, their land, and nature in deep ways we can only imagine. They were connected; they had a sense of place.

Perhaps this is what we all find attractive about the Dudley Farm. It draws us all there for various personal reasons but one thing is sure; it's there that we feel a sense of place. Whether it is a room in the farm house, the gardens, or the farm in its entirety, most visitors express a feeling of being somehow connected and comfortable there. While there they find a peaceful refuge from the modern world.

The comment most often expressed to docents by visitors on tours of the house is that they feel they are home and that they feel strongly connected to it. The same can be heard from those visiting the grounds of the farm as well. It's fun to watch the faces of people as they visit - they are almost always smiling. Why does the Dudley Farm cause such a reaction?

When we visit the Farm, it becomes clear. The Dudley Farm brings us back to a different time and a chance to see and feel what the Dudley's experienced every day. It is literally a doorway to the past. The traffic may roar by and the modern world may intrude in numerous ways, but the overwhelming sense of the past and all it represents to each of us is there. The porch on the house beckons, the barns, gardens, and fields call. We are for a little while in a refuge, we are connected, we have a sense of place.

Chapter Two
The Gift

The value of a man resides in what he gives
and not in what he is capable of receiving.
— ALBERT EINSTEIN

Part One

When David Dudley was born in 1909, he became part of a four generation household on a farm he was destined to become the last occupant. Together with his brother Erastus Irwin, who was a year older, they must have been the focus of attention in the big rambling fourteen room house on the rise overlooking the Durham Road. David's great grandparents and grandparents perhaps saw his birth as the continuation of their proud tradition of farming the land that had been in the family for generations. In the young child they would have seen the future and they, no doubt, would have smiled and watched over his every sound and movement as only those who are assured that their legacy would be preserved could.

David's parents, Nathan (1881-1963) and Amy (1878-1967), were respected and active members of the North Guilford community and the Dudley home was often the center of the social life that bound the farm families of the area together. They too would have looked at their new young son with confidence in the future not knowing the tremendous changes that would engulf them and their farm as the new century their boy had been born into progressed. As Nathan and Amy settled into the rhythms of their daily lives with a second son they surely looked to the future with confidence and pride.

By the time David died in 1991, change had certainly come to the farm of his ancestors. David, who had never married, lived a simple and frugal life alone in the big white house for twenty four years following the death of his mother in 1967. His brother Erastus died in 1950 and his father in 1963. During those years David continued to go about his business as the world around the farm rapidly changed. The second half of the 20th Century saw North Guilford, like the rest of the town, dramatically transformed into a modern suburb as the relentless grasp of developers gobbled up land. Guilford had become a desirable location for the new commuter culture sweeping across the Shoreline of Connecticut and surviving farms were swallowed up as subdivisions sprouted where corn had once grown. Yet David's farm seemed immune to it all; an island of constancy in that torrent of change.

David had lived a life of little fanfare, first as a machinist and later in life as an assistant to a local veterinarian. Though many people knew him it seems very few actually got to know him. David's quiet, shy, and reserved nature masked a dry Yankee wit and a very private life that was in many ways a throwback to all those who had lived on the farm before him. Although he kept a large vegetable garden, Dudley never farmed the land as his father had. The great adventure of his life was his service in the U.S. Army during World War II during which he received a Purple Heart for wounds suffered while fighting in Europe. How much that experience influenced his life choices upon his return is uncertain, but from all indications he was a man content with his place in the world and his life on the farm that had always been his home.

During the latter part of his life, Dudley's circle of family and friends shrank. He continued to care for the farm his family had called home for six generations before him and for many in the growing community of North Guilford he and his farm became living icons of a disappearing past. Oblivious to it all, he tended to his chores and tinkered in the great gray barn as traffic droned continuously on the always busy Durham Road just beyond the fading white picket fence that seemed to keep it all at bay. Those who stopped to visit or just to chat with him found him to be polite but reserved in the finest New England tradition.

After his mother Amy's death, her son closed off most of the rambling old house and lived in primarily three rooms towards the rear. What had been the farm office of his father, the dining room, and the kitchen of the original 1844 section of the house became his domain. Without central heat and with minimal electricity and plumbing, David lived a rather simple lifestyle more in line with that of his 19th Century ancestors than his 20th Century neighbors. He cooked and heated with a wood stove in the kitchen and washed dishes in a simple cold water sink. His mattress was filled with straw and his bed was in the room where his father and grandfather had conducted the business of the once prosperous farm.

Anecdotes about David best reveal the old Yankee qualities of his personality and lifestyle. One of his relatives once told a story of how on occasion she would make homemade clam chowder and bring it up to him. David, she said, would always look at her with dismay and with a twinkle in his eye adamantly refuse to accept the offering saying he could not possibly eat it. After all, David would explain, he always cooked a chicken and vegetables on Sunday and that would always be enough to last him the entire week. He always insisted he would never be able to "fit it in". After a bit more prodding, he would ultimately relent as she left it "just in case" and when she returned later to pick up the dish he would grudgingly admit the chowder was great.

Another relative explained how as a young girl she would occasionally visit David with her parents. She recounted gazing in wonder at what seemed to her hundreds of wishbones hanging from strings strung across the kitchen ceiling. Apparently David thought it bad luck to throw them away and saved them for the times a young visitor might arrive. He always took one down, she said, and together they would try their luck. She could never figure out why she ended up with the larger section and thus all the luck while David would gleefully chuckle saying maybe he'd be the fortunate winner next time.

But David's luck did run out in 1991 and after a brief hospitalization he died. Having no direct heirs, he, in a surprise to the entire North Guilford community, left his money and farm to the North Guilford Congregational Church and the North Guilford Volunteer Fire Company. His reasons were never known but those two pillars of the community were perhaps singled out as organizations that best embodied the traditions his family for so many generations had upheld; a sense of service and commitment to neighbors and friends. Having led a rather reclusive life, he never belonged to the church or joined the fire company so his decision seemed at first a mystery. But, in retrospect, it was as if he was speaking for his ancestors; reaching across time to give a gift that might stem the tide unleashed by the rush of the 20th Century to preserve what he felt was the essence of what the community of North Guilford had once been.

David's gift could not have come at a more critical time when it came to the loss of farmland and open space in Guilford and the region. The construction of the national highway system started in the 1950's by the Federal Government stimulated a period of rapid suburbanization and growth beyond the traditional urban centers throughout the country and Connecticut and its sleepy New England towns were not excluded from this historic cultural and social shift. At first the growth in housing and the commercial development that came to mark the expansion of this era had been largely confined to the environs around Guilford proper as Interstate I-95, known locally as the Connecticut Turnpike, cut a swath through the town from west to east just north of the town center on its way to Rhode Island, Boston, and beyond. Part of an interstate road network that would link the east coast from Florida to Maine, it stimulated a tremendous migration out of the cities all along its path into the new suburbs that exploded into existence facilitated by the ease in travel the road with its automobiles brought. Small farm towns like Guilford became seemingly overnight, bedroom towns for urban business areas previously out of reach. These new residents could now work in New Haven or as far away as New York then return nightly to the quiet and cozy suburb the town had become. With this suburbanization came commercial development designed to provide services for these new inhabitants and quickly old thoroughfares such as the Boston Post Road (Route 1), became meccas for shopping for these increasingly car dependent residents.

Farms that had once graced the shores of Long Island Sound, some whose families had worked the land for generations, were suddenly worth more to their owners as a commodity to sell to a developer than to continue the struggle of making ends meet farming. As the craze swept through the town as elsewhere throughout the nation, the fields that had once grown crops now sprouted tidy new homes for the new inhabitants. They had been drawn to Guilford for its quaint New England charm and rural character; the very things their increasing numbers threatened to destroy.

During this early phase, North Guilford, still remote and rural, escaped the bulk of the change. During the 1960's and 70's however, development methodically crept north from the town center up Route 77 towards the traditional boundary with North Guilford, Route 80. In the early 1980's it began to spill over. Just as it would in thousands of rural communities across the nation during the last two decades of the 20th century, growth in the form of subdivisions began to arrive. The farms and open spaces of the bucolic community were now squarely in the sights of the entrepreneurs who promised Guilford tax revenue and a new vision of the future while offering to new residents a real slice of the American Dream.

James Howard Kunstler in his article, "Home From Nowhere" that appeared in the *Atlantic Monthly* online edition in September 1996 captured for many Americans, including it turns out some from North Guilford, their reaction to the increasing miasma of sprawling development. The fear Kunstler declared, was that the sprawl begot of fifty years of prosperity driven by an insatiable desire to possess material comfort driven by a reliance on the automobile was destroying in countless communities the very cultural fabric that had made them unique.[1] This, Kunstler said, had resulted in an endless series of suburban repetition and mediocrity.

In "Home From Nowhere", Kunstler acknowledged that many Americans had begun to recognize that something had happened to the places we live and work and go about our lives daily. The cookie-cutter neighborhoods devoid of character and charm, the repetitive series of strip malls with their acres of parking lots, the giant box stores, and national franchise restaurants and stores had all resulted in an inimical sameness across the region and nation. This unhappiness expressed itself for many as a significant alienation from the community and disconnect from the cultural and historical heritage that had shaped it over the years. In essence, people were losing their sense of place.

For the members of the Fire Company, the church, and the curious of North Guilford, a growing reaction to the threat of growth was often less pronounced and certainly more subtle. Sure they were witnessing change around them, just look at the crowded classrooms at Melissa Jones Elementary School or the increasing frequency of fender benders on the twisted country lanes of the community. Yet many welcomed new development and for those with land to sell, there was a fortune to be made from land that was increasingly useless for any crop but houses. But for some, there was a nagging sense they were losing something valuable; that rural and historic character that made North Guilford what it was. It was going fast and they all sensed it. That character, rooted in the land and the traditions that had grown from it, was increasingly threatened as each farm and woodlot disappeared. It had been a slow process over the last fifty years, but now it seemed a tidal wave of change was engulfing them.

Part Two

David's gift immediately became the talk of North Guilford and at the Fire House and the Little Store on the Durham Road it was all the buzz. Speculation was mixed with astonishment at the church hall and the school playground. "He did what?" "He gave everything?" "Do you know why?" It was an extraordinary gift; David Dudley, the quiet, gentle man whose farm was familiar to all had given his family homestead and savings to the North Guilford Congregational Church and the North Guilford Volunteer Fire Company. The scope of the gift was startling and though welcomed by both venerable institutions created immediate problems. The value of the property on the corner of routes 77 and 80 would be a developers dream and generate a substantial sum from its sale. David's bank account alone, the accumulated savings of generations, would be a much needed boost to both groups as they were always strapped for funds. But...

For the members of the Fire Company, news of the gift spread faster than an alarm for a burning house. Could there be a mistake was replaced with discussion about the sudden windfall and what it meant and how it might be spent. Perhaps a new truck and equipment? What about an addition to the always crowded firehouse and a training facility? As the group met and the officers discussed the gift, it became obvious that although a wonderful opportunity for the company, some began to question the impact it might have on the organization.

The North Guilford Fire Company No. 4, had been formed fifty years earlier as an all volunteer department to provide fire protection and emergency service to the growing but still sleepy farm community. The residents of North Guilford had a tradition of taking care of their own going back to the days of Cohabit and the Fire Company was the latest manifestation of that sense of community responsibility and service. Like the militia of old colonial North Guilford, it consisted of volunteers who trained together, responded when needed, and elected its officers. They learned to depend upon each other in dangerous situations that were often life threatening and through the common struggle to save lives and property formed a bond not unlike their militia forbearers.

William Dudley waited impatiently outside the small sturdy meeting house on the crest of what had come to be known as Long Hill. As he waited for the rest of the company to muster for their monthly training, he couldn't help thinking back to those early days when together they had established a community out of the area long called Cohabit. He recalled with pride the day his peers had chosen him captain of their newly formed militia and how though with little formal training, he had assumed command with all the enthusiasm he brought to his other positions within the now prospering settlement. Though it was now twenty five years since their trek northward from Guilford village in 1712, it often seemed like only a few days had passed since they were erecting homes together, shaping the timbers from their own lands into sturdy houses and barns. But now, as he stood with his neighbors; the Bartletts, Bentons, and Fowlers, he was overwhelmed by a sense of accomplishment and pride only men like he and his neighbors could feel—a sense of connection to something more important than themselves that they had built together. North Guilford Parish was indeed their home and they all would sacrifice everything if necessary to keep it safe.

Hence the problem: The Fire Company was a nonprofit organization funded through tax dollars from the town for items such as equipment and training; how would David's gift impact all that? Furthermore, would the money be swallowed by the town and the Guilford Fire Department which Company No. 4 belonged? Other than new equipment and training needs—what might the funds be used for? What effect would David's gift have on membership? Would it result in paid personnel? Would members, already hard to find and keep, stop volunteering as the needs of the company changed due to his generosity? The needs and desires of the North Guilford Congregational Church, the Fire Company's partner in the gift, also needed to be addressed. Some sort of settlement with the best interests of both parties and the greater North Guilford community would have to be worked out. But what?

By the summer of 1992, discussions with the Church soon revealed that they would be better served by accepting the savings portion of David's gift. The idea of having to deal with the property and all it entailed was more than the small congregation was willing to tackle despite the possible greater sum generated by a sale. In September an agreement was reached and the Fire Company gave up its claim to the $300,000 monetary component of Dudley's will in return for sole ownership of the property. This relieved the Fire Company of their most pressing dilemma; whether or not such a large cash donation was in their best interest and even feasible. But by agreeing to accept the property at the corner of routes 80 and 77, the Fire Company was now on uncharted waters. What would the best use of the property be? Would a sale in the end be in the best interest of the company and the community?

Wrapped around and through the debate that raged at the Fire House was another issue, one often discussed and usually lamented. It was the rapidly changing nature of North Guilford and the toll in the minds of many being taken in farm land and open space; sprawl. How would the character of the community change if the land was sold off in parcels and houses or a shopping area replaced the farm? There was no denying that North Guilford had changed. Farms, woods, and fields were being replaced with houses and roads, as the many new residents, drawn to the idyllic character of the area, were by their very presence transforming it and diminishing the very thing that had brought them. Many of the new homes were large and the owners commuters, and the sense of community that had typified the region was disappearing. With a strong belief that the rural, farming traditions that for so long had been the hallmark of the community were vanishing the Fire Company members knew that what happened to the farm might be significant. Here they agreed, was an opportunity.

Jehiel Evarts raised his hand to shield the sun as he looked west up the hill toward the main path that led north. He quickly recognized the man as he approached—Captain William was coming to pay him another visit. If anything thought Jehiel, he was persistent. But that persistence was tempered by a strong sense of friendship and fellowship. After all, they had known each other since childhood, had grown up together and had helped open up and settle North Guilford over thirty years before. They knew one another as only men who had lived a common destiny could.

"What say ye Jehiel" shouted the Captain when he saw his friend pause from his late winter plowing. It had been a relatively mild, dry winter and many in the settlement were being given a chance to do some early plowing to prepare their fields despite it being the first week of March.

"It is work I am about, Captain; for I must keep these hands to the plow not being a wealthy man such as thyself" answered Evarts with a grin. "But my beasts can use the rest not having worked since our timbering was done this January past" he said as he patted the closest of his two Devon oxen who had lumbered to a halt. He knew what William wanted—the parcel of land with his dwelling house on it.

Like many of the other planters in North Guilford, Jehiel owned this as well as other lots dispersed throughout the parish, Guilford, and even surrounding towns. This piece was special however; 27 acres cresting a ridge overlooking the West River, some of the best crop land around. On it also sat at the time one of the first and oldest dwelling houses in North Guilford, dating back to the earliest days of Cohabit. It was small, only two rooms, but it was surrounded by a stone and wooden wall in the tradition of the earliest part of the last century; a messuage in the old words of their English grandfathers who first settled Guilford. A house surrounded by a walled courtyard, it had been built to protect the northern reaches of the town sixty years ago along the old Indian path that followed the West River south.

William Dudley had become one of the larger land holders in North Guilford by 1746. At the time of his death in 1761 he held more than 500 acres in the area and had already sold or given to his heir's lands in Guilford, Killingworth, Middletown, and other communities as far away as Litchfield. Through hard work and diligence, the Captain had accumulated land holdings that represented wealth. Hay fields, crop land, meadows, and timber lots were the true mark of a man's worth in the eyes of God and the community and William's showed he was certainly one blessed.

Now, as he had done at least three times over the past year, Jehiel knew his friend was again about to make his offer.

"Aye, 'tis fine soil you till my friend" Dudley said as he approached. "I can smell the blessings of the Lord in the sod". William paused and reached down to grasp a newly turned clump of soil near the iron tipped wooden blade of the plow. "It is truly the work of the Lord that allows us all to till the earth to provide us with his bounty".

"Tis indeed friend" answered Evarts. "But you did not halt my work to comment on the Lord's blessings William. Have you come again to harry me about my land?"

With that the Captain smiled and said "An old friend knowest the truth in the other. You know my quest. I come to make an offer to ye for this fair field and tenement. It will tie together my holdings along the river just south of here which lyeth bounded by that of thee along the other bank of the stream".

Jehiel recalled how William had purchased of the widow Elizabeth Stone the 5 acre lot along the west side of the stream known as Captain Ward's Sawmill place a year and a half past. Since he owned the land south, west, and east of that lot, his Evarts knew, would tie it all together and give his old friend control of lands on both sides of the river and the path north to Durham.

Evarts also knew the Captain had plans to pass on this large parcel to his third son Jared, who in many ways was the picture of his father in stature but not character. Though a respectful and devout man, the young man lacked his father's warmth and diplomatic flair for leadership and camaraderie. But that was not his concern Jehiel thought, but that of the Lord's whose works were revealed through each and he knew in time the young Jared would rise to a position of respect in the community like that of his father.

"William, the persistence of thy mission dost try my patience" said Jehiel with a laugh. "Let us walk to my dwelling and talk of earlier times when our bones did not ache until warmed by the sun and you and I viewed the world through the eyes of young men".

"It is through the eyes of a young man I still do see Jehiel though age has brought prudence and restraint to my view" replied William. "But to

visit the past is to dwell on the works of the Almighty and to do that I will gladly agree".

As Evarts led William towards his modest home he knew that soon he would be moving to his larger house in Guilford now occupied by his son John.

Interlude Number Two

(The following poem appeared in the Dudley Farm newsletter Farm News, *Winter/Spring 2000. Written by Guilford poet Katrina Van Tassel, she describes the Farm during the summer of 1999).*

Dudley Farm , Summer 1999

Weary of the spinning world around me
and beyond I drive seven rolling miles
to the old white farmhouse resting
in an unpretentious setting of ancient
maples a soft hillside deep
near view and distant things to touch
a black cat crossing the driveway
things I cannot see but know exist
beyond the trees the huge car-bed
filled with the Munger Barn numbered
pieces of a gigantic puzzle await
the fitting together the raising
Then oh then what plans lie ahead
for its second lifetime
But first a barn offers its vast silence
Its loftiness its fragrance its
ageless age velvet boards dotted
with old nailheads rafters bearing
such weight with seeming ease
Peace itself
Then enter the dancers poets actors
artists with them the listeners
viewers partakers gathered together
under one roof recalling the not-so-distant
lowing of cattle chitter-chatter of
chickens a dog's bark sheep bells
all awaiting lovers of country history
  Who make possible the dream

Chapter Three
Captain William's Legacy

The greatest use of life is to spend it
for something that will outlast it.
— WILLIAM JAMES

Jehiel Evarts did sell his parcel to his persistent friend. In Volume 7 of the Guilford Land Records, page 66, the transaction was recorded for all to see. It states that Jehiel Evarts, on March 19, 1746 sold to William Dudley:

For One Thousand pounds current money of the old tenor—one messuage or tenement situate lying and being in Guilford aforesaid, in the Parish of North Guilford being the Messuage or tenement where I now dwell, containing by estimation twenty seven acres and three quarters be it more or less as it lyeth butted and bounded Easterly by the West River, southly by land of Daniel Fowler and westerly by land of Daniel Fowler and northly by the highway with a dwelling house thereon standing. [1]

The Evarts parcel was added to William's extensive list of properties and became just one more piece in his quest to extend his holdings, an activity that he continued until his death. The tradition in New England well into the 18th Century was for a father to hand down to his male decedents, both sons and grandsons, parcels of land unlike the practice of primogeniture seen in England at the time where only the oldest male inherited the family property. During the 17th and 18th centuries in Connecticut and the rest of New England, there was still enough land available to follow the more generous custom, a practice that would change by the early 19th Century. William, like other colonial patriarchs, was obsessed with the accumulation of property knowing that the more he possessed the more secure his family would be when his life ended. As a result, Captain William Dudley eventually held title to property throughout North Guilford, Guilford, Branford, Middletown, Killingworth and even in new lands being opened in faraway Litchfield. He and his neighbors also continuously parlayed their holdings with one another in their continuous game of acquisition.

When William Dudley died in the spring of 1761, his entire estate was inventoried as was the custom of the time. Executors went through his home room by room recording what was in each and estimated the value of all items found. All property that he held title to was listed as well. At that time he held 10 different parcels totaling 357 acres. Following the custom of the time, by the time of his death many of his other holdings had been given to his surviving sons Asahel, Medad, and Jared. Asahel was given his land in Middletown and Medad his "... homefarm and all the buildings and all the land I have at Branford...". At the time of the Captain's death, his youngest son Jared was already residing on, as the inventory states, a "...farm that Jared Dudley lived on with buildings—101 acres—fruit trees".[2] This parcel included that bought from Jehiel Evarts and another lot on the east side of the road north to Durham known as Hooker Hill. Together this property would form the basis of what would come to be known as the Dudley Farm.

An interesting side note to the will of Captain William Dudley is that in it he gave two of his grandsons, Dudley and Abraham Baldwin, 50 acres of land in Killingworth in an area called Black Rock. Abraham Baldwin would go on to become one of Guilford's more prominent sons when he represented the state of Georgia at the Constitutional Convention in Philadelphia and signed the Constitution. Baldwin was the son of William and Ruth Strong Dudley's (fifth child and second daughter, Lucy (1721-1758) who had married Michael Baldwin. Abraham graduated from Yale in 1772 and then studied theology at the college and received his license to become a minister in 1775. Instead he served as a tutor at the school until he resigned in 1779 to enter the army as the Revolutionary War intensified. He had already been serving as the chaplain for the Second Connecticut Brigade since 1777 and he continued in the position until the War's end in 1783. Following the War, Baldwin was admitted to the Connecticut Bar but soon relocated to Augusta, Georgia in 1784. He was elected to the Georgia House of Representatives in 1785 and helped to found the University of Georgia where he served as president from 1786 until 1801.

Abraham represented Georgia as a member of the Continental Congress in 1785, 1787, and 1788 and served as a delegate to the United States Constitutional Convention in 1787. Baldwin was then elected to the first five Congresses under the new Constitution (1789 -1799) and continued to serve Georgia in the U.S. Senate from 1799 until his death in 1807. He was chosen to serve by his peers in the Senate as President Pro Tempore during the Seventh Congress. As a legacy, his grandfather William could not have been prouder than to have a descendent with as distinguished career of service as that of Abraham.

At the Fire House, the meetings and talk continued. Now faced with what to do with what was now being called the "Dudley Farm", a new idea became more widely accepted: the farm should be preserved as a farm. But this option opened up a whole slew of new problems the most pressing and important of which was how to go about doing it. Discussion quickly turned to whether or not the farm should be rented out to a tenant who would be willing to work the land and what to do with the rental income that would be generated. What repairs needed to be done to the rambling old farmhouse just to get it into a livable condition for a tenant and a possible family? What about liability? Was this really something the all-volunteer company was actually willing or able to do?

According to a national study released in 2007, farmland loss has reached an epidemic proportion across the United States. Between the years 1982 and 2007, 23,163,500 acres of agricultural land were lost to development representing an area the size of Indiana.[3] Of that total, the small state of Connecticut lost 45,300 acres or roughly one seventh of its total farm land.[4] *LandThink*, a land preservation advocacy website, blames this loss clearly on American's desire to live in low density suburbs[5] of the type that were being built in Guilford in the 1980's and 90's where lots were minimally sized at two, four, or more acres to accommodate the desire of the new relatively affluent residents to surround themselves with the amenities associated with open space. This process, driven by market demand, quickly accelerated during this period as older residents sold their only real asset, their land, at windfall prices assuring a more secure financial future for themselves and their families. This was a local issue and a national dilemma; were our farms and open spaces worth saving?

A study published by the University of Connecticut echoed the sentiment of many across the nation as well as those gathering at the Fire House that autumn when it stated there is a growing worry over the impact of sprawl on the economic, environmental, and cultural character on local communities.[6] A survey of state residents conducted by the university in conjunction with the University of Delaware also published in 2007 revealed that Connecticut residents clearly valued the non-market benefits of farmland preservation and the amenities associated with it in regard to recreation, scenic vistas, and the character of their community.[7] In 1991 the Fire Company members knew that farming on the scale of the past would never return to North Guilford, but motivated by what they saw as a vanishing cornerstone of their community that represented that past, they became eager to preserve it if they could. The Dudley's farm needed to be saved, if not for farming, then at least for the sake of what it meant to residents as a link to that disappearing agricultural heritage.

Like their fathers and grandfathers had done in the past, the Fire Company turned to their neighbors in the North Guilford community for help. Legal advice was sought from local lawyers and politicians were contacted to help guide and advise the Fire Company through the bureaucratic process of saving the Dudley Farm. Soon it was apparent that the first step in the process of preservation was to create a nonprofit entity that would then be able to manage and oversee the property no matter what the final use would be. To that end, the slow legal process of creating a nonprofit organization began even though the ultimate mission of how to use the farm was still unclear. One thing was clear however; the Dudley Farm needed to be saved for present and future generations. What form that preservation would take was not.

A committee of Fire Company members was created to begin the process and they quickly reached out to those in the community who expressed their eagerness to help. It soon became a local crusade of sorts as local residents got wind of what was happening and wanted to assist in any way they could. This in itself became a problem, as questions of how to manage this community outpouring of support began to overwhelm the committee. Pleased with such a response, the committee turned to what had always been a way of reaching out; they began to plan for an open house where the curious could come and view what was now being called a community treasure. But before such an event could take place or the process of preservation could begin, the farm property would have to be assessed and this for all involved was a bit of an eye opener. As the committee gathered by the weathered gray barn one Saturday morning in the early spring of 1993, the anxious banter of anticipation was quickly replaced with the more cryptic comments of pragmatic and experienced eyes as the tour began. Beyond the fading white paint, peeling green shutters, and the worn asphalt roof, there was an old house more suited for burning in a department drill than saving as a home. Yet something came over them as they wandered through the dusty rooms, gazed at the peeling wall paper and surveyed the dirty floors. The past was tugging at them, pulling them in, and taking hold. The chatty bravado of the committee soon took on a solemn almost church-like quality. They knew what they had to do.

When Captain William Dudley died in 1761, he was a well-respected and wealthy man. Yet his life was not without the many heartbreaks and traumas of the age. A brief look at his immediate family and what befell them illustrates how fleeting and tenuous life was during the 18th Century. William, like his neighbors, was a deeply religious man. This was not out of conviction or even choice, but out of an understanding and belief in the uncertainty and frailty of human existence. The grandson of Puritan colonists who had come to New England out of religious conviction, William Dudley was a devout man who clung, along with his family, assuredly to the comforts and answers their church and its teachings provided. They lived and practiced their faith daily with the certainty that all that happened or would happen was the will of the

God they looked to for guidance and solace. The death of a loved one was part of the plan they believed their Lord had created since the beginning of time and in each, though painful, was a lesson and a gift from God that mere mortals might not grasp.

In *The History of the Dudley Family,* a late 19th Century compilation of the many descendants of the first William and his wife Jane who came to Guilford in 1639, a brief biography of Captain William and listing of his family members exists. In it are the names, birth, and death dates of the Captain, his two wives, and children. Of the ten children born to his first wife, Ruth, five predeceased William and three Ruth, who died on September 18, 1743 the victim apparently of disease and she was tragically followed soon after by two daughters, Lois (age 20) and Sarah (age13) on October 7th. It's hard to imagine the sorrow and pain William felt watching helplessly as his wife and daughters died in such quick succession.

In a time when deadly contagious diseases could spread quickly through a community with little hope of treatment other than prayer, the experience of the Dudley family that fall was far from uncommon. Typhus, Diphtheria, Small Pox, and Tuberculosis were just a few of the scourges that took their toll. Like all communities of the time, the women of the family were the care givers during these reoccurring bouts and often became the unwilling victims or carriers of the latest malady to strike. This was probably the cause of the deaths of Ruth and her children.

This was not the first time a multiple tragedy had struck the Dudley family. In the spring of 1733, William and Ruth also lost two children in less than three weeks; their oldest and first child, Submit (age 20), and son William (age 16). Young William had been named for his father and an earlier brother who had died at the age of two in 1717. It's hard to imagine how William must have felt as he looked upon their surviving children, Asahel, Lucy, Medad, Jared, and Mabel with his wife and two daughters now gone that fateful autumn in 1743.

Six years to the day of Ruth's death, William Dudley married Rebecca Fisk, a widow living in Killingworth. It was not uncommon for men or women to remarry following the death of a spouse during the 17th and 18th Centuries as the presence of both a male and female adult was necessary for the proper function of a household. In an age of clearly defined economic roles, men and women were codependent as each performed specific tasks associated with the survival of the family. Women performed the daily tasks associated with food production and cooking, washing, cleaning, and child rearing. They also were responsible for clothing production and repair as well as the planting and maintenance of the family vegetable garden which provided the family with much of their yearly food supply. Males on the other hand, tended the crops, livestock, woodlots, hay fields, meadows, outbuildings, and fences needed for the family income. They may have also practiced a trade such as being a potter or cooper. This clear delineation of labor made 17th and 18th Century households highly productive and efficient. Children as young as five of both sexes also participated in the gender specific work and were expected to assist the adult parent in their daily activities. Thus, the death of a spouse disrupted the entire pattern of work and survival within the home and consequently a new partner became a rather immediate necessity.

When men lost their wives in the 18th Century, an all too frequent occurrence due to the risks of childbirth, illness, and household accidents, they tended to quickly remarry. The fact that Captain William waited six years is interesting in that amount of time was not the norm. This may have been due to the fact that his two surviving daughters, Lucy and Mabel were still at home and able to take on the daily responsibilities of maintaining the household. All this must have changed with the pending marriage of Lucy to Michael Baldwin. Widowers, according to custom, tended to marry younger women and this was the case with William Dudley who at age 65 married the 49 year old widow Rebecca Fisk. Although custom would have allowed Dudley to marry a much younger woman than Rebecca, it appears he opted for a more mature woman beyond child bearing age as a helpmate out of the need for mutual dependence and comfort. Rebecca (1690-1782), would outlive her second husband by twenty two years and remain in part of the house she shared with him until her own death at age 92.

William and Rebecca made what would be called a prenuptial agreement prior to their marriage stating how she would be cared for in the case of her surviving her new husband. The type of arrangement specified was usually found in a will of the deceased male but in this instance Rebecca, having already experienced widowhood, realistically wanted to be assured of her situation in the future. The agreement, called an Indenture, was reprinted in the local newspaper *The Shoreline Times*, in 1901. In it Rebecca would retain use of a portion of their home for the rest of her life and be supplied with certain rights and commodities as well. It stated:

This indenture made this 18 day of September A.D.1749 Between Capt. William Dudley of Guilford in ye county of New Haven & Colony of Connecticut in New England on the one part & Rebecca Fisk late of New Milford now a resident in Killingworth in ye county of new London widow on ye other part Witnesseth that whereas there is a marriage by ye Grace of God shortly to be consummated and solemnized Between the sd. William Dudley & ye sd. Rebecca Fisk, ye sd. William Dudley on his part doth covenant to and with ye sd. Rebecca Fisk, her heirs Executors &c. that if he ye sd. William Dudley die after Coverture with ye sd Rebecca. Before the sd Rebecca, then the sd. Rebecca shall have the use of the Ground Front Room in ye south end of his Mansion House. The use of ye oven and such Part of ye Cellar as she shall have Occasion for, also ye use of ye Well & convenient place for laying wood, and liberty of passing and repassing for ye full enjoyment of ye premises.[8]

I also give to ye sd Rebecca One good Milch Cow, & I also oblige my heirs Executors or Administrators to provide for ye same Pasture in summer & hay in Winter & likewise ye use of a Horse to ride to Meeting and on other Occasions & ye same to be provided for Winter and Summer out of my estate.

Also a sufficient quantity of fire-wood suitable for a fire Yearly & to be Provided by my Heirs Executors &c Sufficient for one fire. I also oblige my Heirs Executors &c to Provide for ye sd Rebecca Sufficient yearly Provision both of Beef and Pork also six bushels of wheat yearly and two of Indian Corn."

All ye above Articles to be provided by my Heirs Executors or Administrators for ye use of ye sd Rebecca During the whole term or so long as she shall remain the widow of ye sd William & do Furthermore covenant to and with the said

Rebecca her Heirs &c to Return all ye Goods Wares Household Stuff Apparrel & Chattels of ye sd Rebecca which I ye
sd William shall be seized or possessed of by Vertue of ye sd
Marriage or coverture and ye sd Rebecca on Her Part for & in
consideration of any fulfillment of ye above written Covenant
doth Hereby Acquitt ye sd William His Heirs Executors and
Administrators All her right of Dower or Thirds by virtue of
sd marriage she might be entitled to, but thereto and therefrom
by virtue of these Presents do fully freely & Absolutely Acquitt
& Discharge ye sd William His Heirs Executors &c.

In this, William Dudley secured for his new wife the security they both
agreed she would need if he predeceased her. A widow's circumstance
could be precarious if not adequately provided for or if she was not
taken in by a relative or child. This solution would have represented a
loss of independence most women would rather not sacrifice and the indenture between Rebecca and William is a strong indication of her desire to remain independent. As William's "relict" as widows were often
called at the time, Rebecca, the indenture states, also had the right to
move into the "Ground Front Room" in the south end of "his Mansion
House" which was a common practice of the time. Although Dudley
stipulated in his will that his homestead and 124 acres with buildings
would go to his second surviving son Medad, it is clear that Rebecca
would, if she chose, share the house with her stepson and his family.

A mansion house, as described in the indenture, was a large home
for the time. Usually a house of this type had a central chimney with a
room on either side on the first floor. The room to the south or sometimes east, was the center of activity in the home called the hall. In
it was done the cooking and food preparation as well as other indoor
domestic activities or work. It was the only room in the house where a
fire might be going most of the day and tended to be the center of all social and economic life. Its southern exposure would make it the warm-
est room in the winter as it caught the first rays of the sun and also
had the most natural light. Opposite the hall was the parlor, a slightly
smaller but more formal room where the family's fancy items and best
furniture were kept. Its fireplace wall was often paneled and the others
painted. The parlor was the ceremonial heart of the house where special

occasions were celebrated and funerals were held. It was the best room, meant to impress guests who were brought in to experience the wealth and good fortune of the family. In some homes of the period, another series of rooms were added across the rear of the house; a central keeping room or kitchen where the cooking and food preparation would have been moved from the hall and on either side of it a small bedroom and a buttery or pantry for the storage of food supplies. Whether the Dudley home had such an addition is not known but the addition of this first floor space would have given the home the typical "saltbox" shape common in New England houses of the early 18th Century.

A mansion house would have had a second floor with two rooms called chambers on either side of the central chimney stack. These were multipurpose rooms used for both storage and sleeping and may have had fireplaces. By the time of the marriage of William and Rebecca, they would have been evolving more into sleeping chambers and when Medad inherited the home they certainly would have been used for that purpose. Access to the second floor would have been from a staircase located in a small room in the front of the house on the first floor called a porch. Located directly in front of the central chimney stack, this small room also served as the main or formal entrance to the home with doors opening to the hall and parlor and a staircase leading to the second floor built against the chimney stack.

When Rebecca died in 1782, she was buried next to her husband with other members of the family in the North Guilford Burial Ground. Her gravestone, typical of the time, was inscribed with brief biographical information and a statement of religious faith. Rebecca's stone is inscribed as follow:

In memory of
Mrs. Rebekah
Relict of the late
Capt. William Dudley
Who died Feb. 9th 1782
Aged 92 years

The inscription that was then carved into the stone gives a bit of insight into the character of Rebecca Dudley. It reads:

This truth how certain
When this life is ore
Saints die to live
And live to die no more[9]

William Dudley's third surviving son, Jared (1727-1811), inherited from his father the land that would become the Dudley Farm. As stated in William's inventory, Jared was already living on the 101 acres that were given to him. Along with Captain Ward's sawmill lot located further north on the Durham Road, and the Evarts property, it would continue to be held by the family through the 19th Century. Jared had married Mary Chittenden (1729-1821) in 1754 and they probably moved at that time into the old Evarts house on what is now Elm Street he was to inherit. At this point no record of another home on the property that would become the Dudley Farm has been found to date but since it has been reduced to 10 of the original 101 acres a location may never be known.

Jared and Mary Dudley had five children, two sons and three daughters and unlike those of his parents, they all survived into adulthood. Their first two children were boys, Luther (1755-1810) and Jared (1757-1843) followed by three girls; Ruth (1762-1846), Eunice (1764-1857), and Mabel (1767-?). Jared followed in the footsteps of his father in many ways as he became a leader in the North Guilford community as captain of the local militia, a title he carried until his death. This position must have been held earlier in his life and may have even been inherited from his father while he still had influence within the community. Records show that he was on occasion referred to by that title but never to the extent William had. Also, by the time of the Lexington Alarm in the spring of 1775 at the start of the Revolutionary War he was no longer active in the local militia in which his son Luther served. Jared was also a landholder of note in North Guilford and land records in the town of Guilford show him both buying and selling property but never to the same extent as his father and only in Guilford or North Guilford. He never acquired close to the same amount of land as William had as economic circumstances changed dramatically during his lifetime.

Although Jared Dudley owned close to 200 acres of land including his home as well as those of his sons, at the time of his death the availability of local property that could be acquired by the last half of his life had declined substantially. This decline was a reflection of population growth, land inheritance practices, and economic decline that began in the 1770's and continued into the early 19th century. Jared continued to be considered a prosperous farmer by local standards though his success was based upon a family economic organization in which his two sons remained tenants on land of their father and the three appeared to work his property for their mutual benefit. The last two decades of Jared's life were undoubtedly filled with increasing economic pressures as competition from more productive and larger farms in New York, Pennsylvania, and the Ohio Valley were making life difficult for farmers such as Dudley throughout Connecticut and New England. With the disappearance of their traditional markets in the growing urban centers of the Northeast and overseas, life became one struggle after another. Many farmers or their family members left to settle new lands to the west or searched for alternatives to farming. Some looked to new crops to survive or a focused on livestock such as sheep but these choices were limited in their ability to reverse the growing trend.

Luther paced the floor of the mill he had come to think of as his own. He thought back to the day when his father had talked of building the gristmill to take advantage of the need neighbors had for one closer to their farms in North Guilford. His father had spoken often when Luther was a boy of the possibility of building the dam on the parcel he had inherited from his father William and starting the milling operation. It was located in a shallow valley formed as the Menunkatuck River wound its way south from Lake Quonnipaug and hit hard against an outcrop of granite. The depression formed by the river over the years as it hit the ledge made an ideal location for the earthen and stone dam that his father Jared had put in place of the broken one made of timbers to store water in a pond to run a wheel. Opposite the stone ledge and stream bed the land rose gently up a low hill to the old cart path that cut north to the lake and Durham beyond and south to the village of Guilford nestled by the shore of Long Island Sound. The old path was quickly becoming the main north/south route and was eclipsing the older road to the east known as Long Hill. It was here Luther's father had said, the family could make their future and so the mill was built.

In those early days the mill was a boon to local farmers and Jared and the family had made a tidy profit grinding their neighbors' corn to flour. But the last few years had been less profitable as demand for local flour continued to drop and the uncertainties of the new American Republic caused economic turmoil across region and the state. Luther paused near the open door and peered across the cart path and thought of the modest house he and his wife Mary shared with their sons on the corner of Long Hill Road and Elm Street. He could not help but feel frustrated by the fact that at the age of 34 and eleven years married he was still living in a house provided by his father on land that was not his own. His father is a good man, a fair man, but he has little sympathy for the aspirations of one with a growing family. Now with his sixth son, Oliver born, Luther was feeling more and more pressure to make a change and strike out on his own. But this mill was his responsibility and he kicked the door a bit more ajar as he thought of how it still paid his father well enough in corn and flour. He knew he could not leave against his father's wishes and move his family west to the Ohio country as many others were. Besides, Mary was a Chidsey and was close to her family and any mention of going west was sternly rejected.

Luther resumed his pacing knowing his father would soon make his Monday morning appearance at the mill. He hated how he would finger the ledger and grimace and mutter as he reviewed it. The comments were always the same and always critical making Luther feel 12 again as if he had once again let the cattle into the cornfield. Why had he been so generous with credit to one neighbor or why hadn't he insisted on a better price for the flour they sold to that sharp witted merchant from New Haven. Always the same; but today, today he was going to stand up and demand a larger percentage of what profits they were still getting. Then he could buy his own land and a larger home for Mary and the boys. He's stuck in the old ways, Luther groused to himself. He needs to understand that things are different now, harder and more complicated.

It began raining heavily again as it had it seemed since November began. The old cart path was awash with mud, more of a March thaw mud than one following a hot dry summer. Soon the last of their neighbors' dried corn from this harvest would be brought to the mill and there would be no more to grind. It had been a poor year as each cart and wagon seemed to bring less than usual for the great stones to turn to flour. The great wooden wheel that caught the water stored from the dam would be put to rest for the season and the grinding stones separated and cleaned. His mood became as somber as the weather and a chill wind blew through the still open door. As he moved to slide it closed Luther glanced up the path to see his father's one horse dray moving slowly in the downpour down the gentle slope and slide suddenly to a stop six rods from the mill.

As Jared dismounted his feet quickly sank in the mire. The right wheel had sunk to the hub and he had an overwhelming desire to curse the god who had created mud. Luther knew as he quickly grabbed his coat and hat that today he would not have that talk with his father. He trudged glumly into the rain and mud.

Interlude Number Three

(The following essay appeared in the Dudley Farm Newsletter Farm News, Spring 2004. In it I wrote about mud as a harbinger of hope though in the 19th Century it was often a constant irritant and obstacle throughout the year depending upon the weather).

The end of winter and early spring was always an exciting and vibrant time on a farm one hundred years ago. Though the landscape saw the last of the snow and ice disappear and the trees still stood starkly barren, the promises of spring were everywhere. During the long cold months, the wood supply for the coming year was cut and stacked to season, fences mended, equipment and tools repaired, and plans for planting made. With the sun rising sooner and setting late, and temperatures moderating, two smells gave hope that spring was on its way; one was manure and the other was mud.

Mud, the eternal forerunner of better weather would begin to appear as the ground froze with the night but thawed with the warming sun. One hundred years ago, as the snow and ice melted and the rains of spring came, farm families often found themselves immersed in it. Lacking the paving and drainage that simplify our lives today, mud was everywhere.

Mud made life a challenge in ways we might find hard to imagine. Following a long winter, it often made roads impassable as poor drainage and maintenance turned them into a quagmire. Wagons might slide and teams of sure footed oxen and horses often slipped on the soft and soggy road beds while elsewhere the thawing process created ruts that grew deeper as the season progressed. Although road maintenance had become common by the end of the 19th Century, equipment in general was ill-suited to handle the degree and depth of the seasonal damage. As roads became soupy bogs with jagged furrows, wagons and carts got stuck, axles and wheels broke, and frustration reigned.

Eager to begin work in their fields, farmers would often occupy their time filling soft spots in their farm roads and cart paths with stone and gravel while ditching and draining kept them busy until their soggy fields began to dry. Muddy fields could not be manured or plowed postponing the promise of planting until dried by the winds and sun of spring.

Farmers knew mud—the smell and consistency of each type was different. Soil content made some sweet and some difficult to smell. The quality of the mud also differed by clay content and water amount so that some were cloddish and thick with clumps while others could suck off the boot of the unwary foot that stepped in it. Some muds were grainy or runny and colors varied from red to black. But despite the nuisance and problems it caused, the promised hope of spring was in each muddy grasp.

Soon the mud would be gone and the work of planting could begin. The cycle of life would continue as the seasons progressed. Fields were plowed and planted, crops were harvested and the cycle renewed. Mud, the harbinger of spring, always announced the start of the cycle.

Today at the Dudley Farm, we know mud as well. As a late 19th farm museum, this time of year it is an ever present reminder of what life on a farm was all about. Mud is everywhere and as winter gives way to spring and the start of another year of activities at the Farm, it wouldn't be surprising to lose a boot or two.

Chapter Four

Genesis

An idea is salvation by imagination.
— FRANK LLOYD WRIGHT

W hat a mess. It was worse than they could have imagined; the dirt, the peeling wallpaper and paint, no furniture, piles of debris - and that was just the house. The big barn and outbuildings were much the same or crumbling due to years of use and neglect but filled with what could best be described as the deteris of 150 years of farm life. But the house and barn were sound for the most part and that was a start. The group, now called the Dudley Farm Committee, sized up the magnitude of their task and agreed to meet again soon. There was much to be done.

When David Dudley died the contents of the farmhouse, as stipulated in his will, went to one of his nephews. The inventory of items listed through the probate court was a snap shot into the history of the farm and the Dudley family since the 17th Century. But even though the house now stood empty which added to the forlorn and abandoned quality of each room surveyed, there was a warmth and charm that was hard to explain as if the home was calling to them to look beyond the dust and faded memories of all those years.

The Dudley Farm Committee reached out once more to the greater community through an open house one brilliant fall Saturday in 1993 where curious neighbors stopped by to see what the Fire Company had.

It became a fair of sorts as neighbors and those who knew of the farm came for a look. Despite the untidy worn condition of the property the reaction of friend and stranger alike was the same; a smile and an expressed sense of comfortableness that the house and grounds gave them. As the farm cast its spell, committee members explained their evolving thoughts and plans for it through tours and chats. With each stroll about the barns or peak into the rooms of the house, onlookers began to voice their support and many did not hesitate to volunteer what they could to help.

Planning began as the Farm Committee met to discuss what to do and how to do it. These sometimes heated discussions began to reveal an interesting dilemma. The Fire Company was a local organization from a different time before North Guilford had begun to grow. As a matter of fact, the Company was approaching its 50th year of existence and many of the founding members were still actively involved. Most of the members were homegrown men; they knew who each other's fathers and sometimes grandfathers were and they knew the strengths and weaknesses, quirks and constants of one another in a way only brothers might. This gave them a solidarity when confronted with a house fire, accident, or any other emergency situation and they possessed a confidence in one another that had been tested over time which allowed them to take on a task, turn to each other for help, and get the job done. But the Dudley Farm was different; here they were in uncharted territory.

Many on the Committee and in the Fire Company had no problem with what they saw as a renovation of the house and barns. Fix her up, rent her out to a young farmer, and keep the farm running. But others saw the need for more; more than just a quick coat of white paint and a fast sprucing up. The issue was the historic nature of the property and how to preserve it. This led to a traditionally sensitive issue. Since the days of Cohabit, residents of North Guilford had always prided themselves on being different and somehow separate from those they saw as more wealthy and cultured in Guilford to the south. It was a feeling of inferiority for some, a sense of rural verses more settled for others, or just a notion that those long eight miles to the town center led somehow to a remote disconnect that had always created a sense of independence and self-reliance. In North Guilford, they had traditionally taken care of their own and the Fire Company was a manifestation of that fact. To the south in Guilford proper they had stores and businesses, historic homes and districts, the green in the center of town and a deep sense of Guilford as an historic old Connecticut town. In North Guilford things were different; they prided themselves on the dust on their boots and the craggy nature of their hills and people. They felt themselves an island of a unique past without the trappings, stuffiness, and money so obvious to them to the south.

As they looked around the fire house and talked about preserving the Dudley Farm in some way as a farm from the past, the committee members realized they lacked the expertise and would have to look beyond the Company for that. This put them nervously in unfamiliar territory but they did not hesitate. Interested outsiders who seemed to have the skills and desire required were brought on board and in the end this proved crucial to saving and preserving the farm.

The first few meetings the fall of 1993 were well attended as scores of interested members of the community made their way to the fire house on Wednesday evenings to be part of the exciting adventure the Dudley Farm had become. But as the meetings became weekly and the weather turned colder, fewer and fewer were able to attend. Some lost interest, some found the possibility of another commitment in their busy lives a bit too much, and others left with an assurance they'd be called when help was needed and work was to be done. The group dwindled to a small core convinced of its role but unsure of exactly what form their mission was to take. But important steps were taken during those early meetings and crucial decisions were made. One was to begin the legal process of creating a nonprofit entity to oversee the Dudley Farm and whatever form its restoration took. Through the volunteer efforts of local attorneys The Dudley Foundation was eventually born, though the pace of its birth was sometimes agonizingly slow. The Farm Committee also transformed itself into a governing board to oversee that eventual Dudley Foundation and chose officers and board members to supervise continued efforts to manage the farm and its evolving development.

One of those interested outsiders was Doug Williamson, a draftsman and designer who was, as a North Guilford resident, steeped in local history. Doug had not hesitated to get involved with the early efforts to save the farm and his enthusiasm and talents soon made him an integral part of the Committee and then board. Having restored the Luther Dudley home, Doug had embraced the history and quirky nature of North Guilford like a native and was a font of information and knowledge when it came to where to go and how to proceed with the historic preservation of the farm. Doug pushed long and hard for the committee to do things right, to honor and preserve the historic character of the house, barns, and land. He also introduced the notion of the Dudley Farm as a community center and resource of sorts, a place where neighbors and friends could gather to rekindle and preserve the sense of community that so many in North Guilford feared was being lost.

It was through Doug that I first became involved with the farm. Among the courses I was teaching at Guilford High School at the time was a class on local history through archeology and another on American History through the study of architecture. Both courses had been embraced by the local Guilford historical community and I was fortunate to conduct archeological digs at various historic homes and properties in the town with the students and use the community as an historic architecture laboratory for the architecture class. The high school principal at the time, Barbara Truex, had been contacted by Doug and she had asked Tom Leddy, the Wood Technology teacher, and I if getting involved with the Dudley Farm was something we might be interested in. We both jumped at the opportunity as Barbara explained how Doug, who was acting as Farm Director on behalf of the Committee, had reached out to the high school with the hope students might be able to become involved in the restoration and preservation of the farm. Two days later the three of us, Barbara, Tom, and myself, made the short five minute drive to the farm from the school not knowing at all what to expect.

It was like stepping through a portal to another time as we began our tour of the house with Doug enthusiastically leading us from room to room in the old worn home. He spoke excitedly of the Dudley's and how they had built and lived on the farm, of David, who's ghost I saw everywhere, and the fire company's plan to restore the farm. As we wandered the warren of empty rooms I was struck by the historic nature of what we saw; a perfect, though shabby survivor of the late 19th century and the incredible possibilities it offered Tom and me to teach students about life in the 1800's in a way no other class might. We had both read many of the Foxfire Books, where a teacher and his students in Kentucky had been able to help preserve much about disappearing rural life while exposing them to the skills and crafts of yesterday. Here we had our own opportunity to not only help preserve the farm, but give students a once in a lifetime chance to learn and practice history in a hands-on way.

As we left the house for a look at the great gray barn, Tom and I nodded to one another, we knew what we'd like to do. But would Barbara go along or be able to spring us and some students free from the bureaucratic shackles that dictate the life of a modern high school? We began to talk excitedly about possibilities with Barbara whose enthusiasm was quickly apparent. Doug could not have been more pleased as we left him standing by the barn waving as David had a few years earlier.

It was warm for late October and the scent of fall hung over the old burial ground despite the heat. Erastus looked sadly at the newly carved headstone that held his father's name. "Luther Dudley". "Born Sept. 16th 1755, Died Sept. 14th 1810". But it was the epitaph below that he could not pull his eyes from, transfixed.

> Bubbles our wasting lives betoken
> The shuttle stops the glass is broken
> And like a stream that passes by
> Is man who only lives to die[1]

It had been ordered carved by his grandfather Jared who seemed to have taken the death of his son as a personal affront. Erastus and his brothers had asked him not to include the poem, but the old man had insisted, so there it was. It seems that even in death, Jared wanted the last word when it came to his son. As he stared at the stone his brothers Loveman and Prosper called out as they passed by the clapboard meetinghouse their great-grandfather had helped to build. They had all agreed to meet and talk of the family's future and all three had agreed the site of their father's resting place a fitting location for they all knew at last he was at peace.

Erastus and his brothers had watched as their father had taken to imbibing in the corn liquor made by neighbors and friends more frequently over the past ten years. They understood how his dreams had been dashed by the realities of life but could not comprehend the melancholy that increasingly enveloped him. Luther had been a good father, Erastus remembered, always attentive and eager to help and advise as he fussed about the gristmill that had become his escape and his prison. Since the time of his youth, he had recognized a sadness and frustration in Luther that he realized grew out of circumstance and a powerless inability to change it.

Erastus and his brothers knew of their father's eagerness to do more with his life and how he felt trapped by Jared's desire to keep him in place for the good of the family. The small two over two room house they had grown up in held few secrets. It was however, the news of their oldest brother Luther's death that really seemed to bring about a change. Lost during a voyage to the South Sea while whaling, it seemed from that time on their father had begun to withdraw into himself and to drink the corn liquor the neighbors brought along with their corn to be milled. Erastus remembered the awful night young Luther had left and the terrible row that had taken place. His brother had proclaimed that he did not want to be trapped as his father was and how he longed for more in life. Shipping out of New London on a whaling bark would give him that chance he said as he stormed from the house to the mournful cries and of their mother, convinced she would never see him again. She was right.

One year later, in 1800, a worn, yellowed letter came from the captain of the ship, delivered over time and oceans from one ship to another until it had arrived in New Haven, expressing his deep sympathy for the loss of their son who had died just three days after the ship had departed for the South Pacific. Stunned, Erastus remembered, his parents had said nothing and his father just walked down the Durham Road to the mill and his elixir. Luther, he knew, blamed himself for his eldest's death, knowing he had been powerless to provide him with the means to make a living on his own. But it was the death of his youngest brother, Frederick, that Erastus knew caused Luther's life to unravel.

Freddy was just sixteen when he joined his brother. He had been unloading sacks of corn to be ground at the mill when the oxen, which stood passively to the front of the cart, were startled and backed it up against the loading platform pinning Freddy between it and the wheel. Luther had dropped his empty jar off the platform, causing the beasts to jump. He blamed himself for his youngest death, and his downward spiral quickened. It was then that Loveman and Erastus had taken over the responsibility of *the mill, knowing as the weeks following Freddy's death turned to months, that their father could not be counted on to work the stones. Luther began to take long walks up the ridges across the Durham Road and often they found him seated atop the one called the Three Monks, for it was from there he could look out to Long Island Sound and the sail he thought would return his oldest son.*

When Luther came down with a bilious fever, the family watched the fight for life leave him. Their mother said nothing yet tended him night and day. Their grandfather had stormed angrily to his son's sickbed, demanding that he get up and return to his business at the mill; as if somehow returning to the life that had broken him would cure him. His last day had been curious; a smile of contentment had enveloped his feverish face until the evening when Luther quietly died, seemingly at peace for the first time in memory. Prosper had been with him and had awakened his mother who had been slumbering in her chair. As always, Mary said nothing, but kissed her husband's forehead and left the room to fix a meal for her boys.

Luther's burial followed quickly after his body had been waked in Jared's parlor at his insistence and Erastus had found it sad how the old patriarch had gazed in disbelief at his departed son mumbling quietly how if only the hand of the lord had been different. But now, here they were, as Loveman and Prosper came to stand beside the marker as well, staring at the freshly carved brownstone Jared had erected, a testimony to their fathers' unfulfilled dreams. His struggle was now theirs and each was determined to see it end differently.

The death of his son may or may not have been the trigger that sent Luther Dudley into a spiral, but it certainly would have been a devastating shock. There is no more poignant message of how Luther and Mary felt than the inscription they placed on their son's gravestone in the North Guilford Cemetery as a memorial following the news of his burial at sea. It reads:

In Memory of
Mr LUTHER DUDLEY
Who left his native shore
29 of Septr 1799 on a voyage to
The Pacific Ocean: and was lost
On the 3rd Day; having just
Entered the 21st Year of his Age.

The poem they had carved on the stone is especially telling:

> Adieu my friends, my parents dear,
> The heaving sigh, the falling tear
> Wilt nought avail; by God's decree
> I slumber in the roaring sea!
> Then humbly bow, and kiss the rod
> Adore and love a sovereign God;
> And let your fixt endeavour be
> To fit for death, and follow me.[2]

Luther Dudley had indeed lived a life of diminished expectations and increasing frustration and in many ways he typified what was happening to many families throughout the region. Land, which had traditionally been the measure of wealth during the past 150 years, had become expensive and difficult to obtain. There just wasn't enough to support the large families and with Jared either unwilling or unable to partition his holdings Luther had been condemned to a life of dependency. With local farms too small and inefficient to compete with those larger more prosperous ones to the west of New England, Luther's small holdings were barely sufficient. Luther remained dependent upon his father for his entire adult life despite the fact that he did own a total of 72 scattered acres mostly used for the maintenance of his livestock. The *1799 U.S. Census* identified Luther as a farmer by occupation and listed his total assets at $206.12 which include the following pieces of real estate:

- 18 Acres of English mowing (hay)
- 6 Acres of pasture
- 6 Acres of boggy meadow
- 8 Acres of fresh and salt meadow
- 30 Acres of bush pasture
- 8 Acres of unenclosed land

72 Acres Total

Luther's personal estate was also listed in the census and it was broken down into two categories; money and livestock. He possessed only 12

"Silver Notes" and $10.00 "money on interest". The livestock was listed as follows:

1	2 yr old Oxen	7	3 yr old Cows
2	2 yr old Cows	2	3 yr old Horses

When Luther died in 1810, his family would have been listed as:

Husband:	Luther Dudley	Age 55
Wife:	Mary Chidsey	Age 53
Son:	Loveman Dudley	Age 29
Son:	Erastus Dudley	Age 27
Son:	Nathan Dudley	Age 25
Son:	Oliver Dudley	Age 20
Son:	Prosper Dudley	Age 17

Predeceased:

Son:	Luther Dudley	(b. 9/6/1779 and d.10/1/1799)
Son:	Frederick Dudley	(b. 1787 and d. 1/18/1803)

Of his three oldest surviving sons, only Erastus had remained in Guilford by the time of Luther's death. The two youngest, Oliver and Prosper would certainly have faced the hard choice of leaving soon as their prospects would have been meager. Oliver would eventually move to Alabama where he established his family and Prosper to Ohio. Loveman had moved to Virginia some time earlier in the decade and Nathan had left in the early part of 1810 for the West, first to the Buffalo region of New York and then later on to Kentucky where he eventually married and started a family. Tragically he drowned in the Ohio River.

Loveman Dudley had apparently returned to Guilford either just prior to his father's death or shortly after, for he does factor into the settlement of his father's estate and is afterward listed in residence in North Guilford. But these were dark days for the family and with few options or resources available to them the conversations held between the brothers must have been earnestly tinged with a sense of desperation. With their grandfather Jared still living, perhaps in time some sort of settlement for the future might be found.

Interlude Number Four

(The following poem appeared in the Dudley Farm newsletter Farm News, *Winter/Spring 2000. Written by Guilford poet Katrina Van Tassel, she describes the dilemma caused by time and the struggle that is waiting).*

The Long View

We celebrate the end of a century
with a golden river of flame towers
of light a sky stunned with firework stars
empty ferris wheels spinning endless designs
the crystal ball falling unscathed
a firm resolution to try to do better
endings are always a bit forlorn but
taking the long view might be the better path
In earlier centuries life was brief moved
at a slower pace packed full to permit
no waste now lifespan stretches to new
longevity and should allow leftover time
to expend where and how we choose
Yet time is never wide enough deep enough
to encompass our yearnings their fulfillment
While we wait for apples to ripen in the orchard
on the side of Bishop's Hill we feel frustration
Why leaves and petals take such endless
time to thrust out hard green globes turning
rosy red juicy edible why not overnight
There is a lesson to be learned from nature's
careful plan nothing haphazard no way
to bypass the order waiting is part of time's
expenditure nature's pattern the unbreakable
rules of the game sequences is everything
from seed to root to blossom to fruit to mouth

Chapter Five

Dreams of Erastus

I have spread my dreams under your feet;
tread softly, because you tread on my dreams.
—William Butler Yeats

Tempers flared. Frustrated and tired, we had been at it since 6:30 that evening and now with the clock approaching ten there was little hope of reaching a resolution. We committee members were trying that spring to somehow develop a plan that would move the restoration of the farm forward. Tensions had begun to develop as early as that past fall of 1993 and now with summer approaching the only thing the group could agree on was to disagree.

The Dudley Farm committee established by the Fire Company over a year ago had evolved into a small core of the company's members and some invited outsiders. Tom and I, having begun a pilot program with high school students at the farm that spring semester were new members, enthusiastic and dedicated but unfamiliar with the nuances of decision making inherent to the Fire Company's culture. The other outsider was Doug, who as the "farm director", had moved into the northern half of the old house while attempting to make it habitable. The costs were running high; electrical work, wall board, and the seemingly thousands of little gotcha's that confounded the task of updating and creating a modern living space from one so outdated and long neglected.

What money the committee had to work with had come through informal fund raising and donations and now it was all but gone. Major repairs needed to be done on the house, the exterior alone needed to be stabilized and painted before another winter's wear might do irreparable harm. Many of the outbuildings were already beyond saving and the big gray barn was starting to sag in more places than the members of the committee were comfortable with. The arrival of the ten hand-picked students who had volunteered to take our first "Dudley Farm Class" had been a shot in the arm to the group and their energy had re-invigorated the restoration effort. But there was a limit to what Tom and I could do with their unskilled but eager hands and the time short of an hour we spent at the farm each school day never seemed enough.

One thing was abundantly clear however; all members were dedicated to saving the farm. But without a well-defined and articulated plan exactly what form it would take and how to go about that "saving" would continue to haunt every meeting and discussion members had. In the end that was the heart of the many disagreements that roiled the now weekly meetings. Not having an expertise in historic preservation or restoration, the Fire Company members were unsure of many of the ideas Doug proposed and at times saw little merit in them. Doug on the other hand, would become impatient with what he perceived as foot dragging delays and road blocks to moving the farm forward as a museum and community resource dedicated to farm life. Then there was the money. There was none.

Every week the financial situation worsened that spring. The process of creating the Dudley Foundation was moving forward at an agonizing pace. The idea of creating what is now that foundation to oversee and operate the farm was seen as imperative in order to alleviate the potential pitfalls and problems caused by the publicly funded volunteer fire company's ownership. The idea was to put the farm into the hands of a nonprofit entity with oversight and ultimate ownership remaining in the hands of the Company. Until the foundation could be established, fund raising efforts were limited and even the idea of membership by donation in a "Dudley Farm" organization had to be tabled. Under these conditions, how does one take on a task as monumental as preserving, restoring, and operating a farm like the Dudley's had created along the Durham Road?

To make matters even more complicated, the residents of North Guilford as well as many in Guilford and surrounding towns, were responding to the news of the attempt to save the farm in an overwhelming fashion. Through telephone calls to committee members and people stopping by the fire house or the farm, individuals and organizations generously expressed their support. Some simply asked how they could help, a few offered to give some money towards the cause, and many wanted to donate household items, farm tools, and equipment they thought might be appropriate. Quickly the big gray barn filled with donated items that mixed with the already existing piles of what could politely be described as a collection of discarded materials and broken equipment that had survived the past 150 years. A system of how to keep track of it all had to be developed and Doug did his best to sort it all out. More important was the need to harness that enthusiastic support in a way that would bring some sense of order to the chaos.

It was becoming increasingly apparent that spring that the committee would need to establish a clear idea as to what the farm would be. Would it be a farm museum? Would it be a community resource and gathering place for the residents of North Guilford or maybe a "North Guilford" museum of sorts? Would it be an educational resource for the local school system or possibly reach beyond? Should the educational mission include the public at large? Should the farm become an environmental center? A cultural center? Should there be membership? The more we talked about a mission for the farm, the more it became clear that exactly what form that mission would take was as varied as the number of people sitting around the table discussing it.

Yet slowly it all began to come together as spring moved to summer and then fall. The committee, headed by Oliver "Buster" Scranton began to move forward as the weather turned warmer and the natural beauty of the farm blossomed. In many ways it was the steady and deliberate leadership of Buster that helped the committee struggle through. A descendent of many of Cohabit's original settlers, Scranton was not only the area's only remaining fulltime farmer, he was also the current chief of the fire company and arguably the most respected member of the community. Since the majority of the committee members, Henry Tichy, Bob Ashman, Don Homer, Joan Stettbacher, and Charlie Hammarlund were all company members, Buster's leadership was at times crucial. Together these members worked tirelessly to make the farm and its preservation happen and from the beginning donated long hours and sometimes days to the basic and sometimes difficult tasks of repairing, installing, and simply fixing what needed to be fixed. Henry and Bob could work on, build, or fix anything and Don, as treasurer of the Fire Company took on the often unpleasant job of monitoring the financial status of the farm. Joan would take on any task asked with an enthusiasm and energy that shamed us all and Charlie's often sage advice proved invaluable.

By the fall of 1994, a vision of sorts began to emerge. Along with Tom and Doug, I pushed to establish the farm as a museum, one that would preserve and reflect the agricultural heritage of the region. This certainly aligned itself with the initial thoughts of the Fire Company members and the idea was embraced by all. The only real issue became what time period to be depicted so that the farm as a museum might gain a historical legitimacy which a hodge podge and random collection of farm items would not. The decision proved easy. The house and barns were a perfect reflection of the late 19th and very early 20th centuries as they had changed little in all the intervening years. With minimal electricity, no central heat, and little plumbing, the house in reality was a perfect, though shoddily preserved, example of that time.

It was also a great choice from the point of view of Guilford. The town already had three long established historic house museums and a fourth was soon to be added. The Dudley Farm would be the fifth. What made the decision to depict the period around the turn of the last century appealing was that it fit perfectly into the sequence depicted by the other museums. There was the flagship property, the 1639 Henry Whitfield House, owned and operated by the State of Connecticut since the late 1890's and the oldest building in town and the oldest stone building in New England. There were also the two long established house museums, the circa 1700 Hyland House, owned and operated by the Dorothy Whitfield Society and the 1776 Griswold House, owned and operated by the Guilford Keeping Society. Both of those organizations had been created to save those structures earlier in the 20th century and are still intensely active in the preservation and depiction of Guilford's history in general. Within a few years the Keeping Society would also begin the process of restoring and opening the Medad Stone

Tavern that would portray the period around 1800.

Guilford, like many towns throughout Connecticut and New England, has a heritage that goes back to the early colonial era. What makes it relatively unique is that a large number of its homes from the 17th through early 19th century still exist which gives it a special charm few other communities can match. Its elegant town green and the tidy rows of old housing stock that line the streets that radiate from it give the town a feeling of timelessness and continuity. This historic fabric and the sense of connection that it represents manifest itself in countless ways in the town's politics, economics, and culture. Above all, a belief in preserving that fabric as a meaningful and important part of the community is pervasive and at times passionately defended.

This made for a curious process of acceptance as the creation of the Dudley Farm evolved during 1993 and 1994. The historic community was definitely interested in what was unfolding north of what had come to be known as the border between Guilford and North Guilford, Route 80. The state highway that bisects the town from west to east had become the defacto dividing line between the two parts of the community and sometimes seemed to enhance rather than diminish the sense of separateness that many in North Guilford traditionally felt. Clearly, the long established historic organizations in Guilford looked at the unfolding process that was the Dudley Farm with an interested but distant eye. This reflected not only the traditional divide between the two regions of town, but a possible grudging disappointment in not being asked to play a greater part. They certainly had adopted a wait and see attitude.

Although individuals within the historic community in Guilford did reach out and offer support, as a group their wait and see approach was a reaction to the fact that although many of them knew Doug and some knew me through my work with them through the school, a clear cultural line was drawn by the Fire Company members of the committee. Fire Company members found it difficult to reach out to those they did not know and their sense of self-reliance born from the cultural traditions of North Guilford and the Fire Company, made them inclined to go it alone. Tom and I had early on experienced this ourselves, as from the start we had been received politely by the other committee members but kept at a distance despite our commitment to help save the farm. We soon learned it was nothing personal, just the way things were. I learned over the years that other outsiders would get the same sense and many would interpret this as a deliberate rebuff of their efforts to become involved.

What the Dudley Farm committee was struggling to save is the direct result of the dreams, ambitions, and hard work of Erastus Dudley. When his father died in 1810, he was 27 years old, the second oldest of Luther and Mary's surviving sons, and the heir apparent to the family's fortunes, or should it be said misfortunes. But at this point the story must return to his grandfather Jared who still held the future of the family in his hands. In 1810 Jared Dudley was 83 years old and the death of his oldest son must have come as quite a blow. By this time he had already written his will so it might be assumed that he was in ill health. In the document which was recorded in the Guilford Probate Records[1] in June 1811, the year of his death, Dudley had named his two sons Luther and Jared as executors. An inventory of his property also recorded that month shows a value of over $5000.00, a substantial sum at the time.

Jared and his wife Mary (Chittenden) had five children. Luther had been their oldest followed by Jared (1757-1843), Ruth (1762-1846), Eunice (1764-1857), and Mabel 1767-?). In his will, Dudley clearly outlined how he wanted his property to be distributed. It reads as follow:

> I give and bequeath to my well beloved wife after my just death and funeral charges are paid, one third of my personal estate to be her own and at her discharge forever, also the use of my desk and clock, and library during her natural life. I give and bequeath to my beloved daughter Ruth Filer in addition to what she had at the time of her marriage, one dollar to be paid by my executors.

Jared then went on to assign to his daughter Ruth's children monetary sums:

> I give and bequeath to my beloved grandson Jared Dudley Filer four pounds lawful money when he shall come of lawful age,

to be paid by my executors. I give and bequeath to my beloved granddaughter Marriah Filer four pounds lawful money when she shall come of lawful age to be paid by my executors. I give and bequeath to my beloved granddaughter Jerusha Filer four pounds lawful money when she shall come of age to be paid by my executors. I give and bequeath to my well beloved granddaughter Parmel Filer and grandson John Filer four pounds lawful money when they shall become of lawful age to be paid by my executors.

His daughter Mabel was included as well:

I give and bequeath to my beloved daughter Mabel Ford in addition to what she had at the time of her marriage twenty pounds lawful money to be paid in five years after my death by my executors.

Eunice, Jared's second daughter was not mentioned. The reason why is curious and can only be speculated on. Eunice had married Jonathan Russell and perhaps there had been some sort of falling out. In the final section of the will, Jared mentions his deceased son Luther and only surviving son Jared. The two are assigned the bulk of his estate following the long established tradition of the father passing on to his sons the land he had worked his entire life to accumulate and retain. Ironically, Luther Dudley finally obtained what in life had always eluded him.

I give and bequeath to my beloved sons Luther Dudley and Jared Dudley to their heirs and assigns forever all my real and divisional estate, not here to fore given after my just debts and funeral charges, and above legacies are paid, to be equally divided among them. Exulting to my beloved son Luther Dudley, I give my clock and right to the library of North Guilford after the death of my beloved wife. And to my beloved son Jared Dudley my desk after the death of my beloved wife. I appoint my well beloved sons Luther Dudley and Jared Dudley to be the executors of this last will and testament...

The will opens an interesting window into the mind and thoughts of Mr. Dudley. It appears that he certainly favored some of his children and grandchildren over others and that his property, which he had jealously husbanded throughout his life would be equally divide between his two sons. With Luther's death, the inheritance made its' way to Erastus.

Assuming that Erastus and his brothers received fifty percent of their grandfather's property to divide among themselves, exactly how that process was carried out is fun to imagine. Of the remaining sons of Luther Dudley, Erastus was the only one who was clearly established with a family in North Guilford at the time of his grandfather's death living in the home of his father Luther that he shared with his mother. Mary had the use of one room in the dwelling. Erastus had married Ruth Fowler in 1806 and by 1811 had two infant daughters. Loveman had recently returned from Virginia, Nathan had left for the West prior to their father's death, and Prosper and Oliver were still considered not of the proper age to strike out on their own.

Jared Dudley's land was inventoried following his death and recorded in the Guilford Land Records[2] on June 25, 1811. It reads as follows:

An inventory of the real and financial estate of Captain Jared Dudley, late of Guilford and made by us the subscribers being first hand according to law. Dates at Guilford June 25th 1811.

The house where the deceased last dwelt, $250.00
the barn and shed near do, $200.00: $450.00
The house where Luther lived,
$200.00 the barn near do $170.00: $370.00
The barn south end of the home lot,
$200.00 the house where Jared lives, $170.00 $310.00
one third of the cider mill,
$170.00 The Evarts lot so called estimated at 28 acres,
$50.00, the hooker hill lot at 5 acres at $19.00: $1665.00
The Nealson lot estimated at 86 acres around 54.00: $432.00
The mill lot estimated at 12 acres at $19.00: $228.00
The Coan lot estimated at 7 acres at $10.00: $70.00
The Fromful hill lot at 44 acres at $14.00: $616.00

The rose meadows at G----s $10.00:	$90.00
One half the area near the house where Luther lived:	$100.00
The major Thompson lot at 30 acres at $40.00:	$1200.00
Two acres and 34 rods salt Marsh $80.00:	$177.00
Jared Dudley's estate totaled	$5408.00.

Assuming it was divided equally between their uncle Jared and the sons of Luther, the portion of the estate inherited by Erastus and his brothers was around $2700.00. By 1812, Guilford town records show Erastus with an estate worth $2000.00. Had he reached a settlement with his brothers?

It was an odd feeling to stand in the door of the mill looking back across the road to the lot he planned to build his new home. How many times had he seen his father do the same? Erastus's mind raced for he knew that change would be coming quickly, but what form it was to take only the Lord knew. He and his brothers had continued to talk about how to best proceed with the family's future and they had agreed that he should continue to work the gristmill while things were settled with their grandfather. Reality was there was not much to do now that it was January and there was no longer any corn or grain to grind. He had felt assured and honored by the men of the community when they expressed their support for him and pledged they would continue to bring him their corn and wheat. In this fast changing world at least you could always count on your neighbors Erastus thought. There was comfort in that and he recalled how the entire community had rallied around the family when his father died, just as they would with a barn raising or any other job or task that needed to get done. Their lives were interwoven for good or ill and the support system was something they could all rely on and integral to whom they were.

A cold breeze chased Erastus back into the mill and he abruptly slid the big door closed. Best to get back to sharpening the stones he thought as he walked back over to the two big stones used to pulverize and grind the kernels into flour. They were old and made of local granite. When sharpened they held a good edge but he had seen the white limestone called burr stone other millers had imported from France. He knew they were beyond his reach as he turned to his task. He had already finished chiseling out the series of groves cut into the base stone, freeing them of the season's buildup of powder and returning them to their original sharpness, ready now for the spring milling of winter rye and wheat. As he turned his attention to the top or runner stone, which had been lifted off the other by the large crane used for that purpose, he mulled over the fact that his future and that of his family lay with this mill and the dam it sat upon. The question was how to move forward. With the new century, despite the many ups and downs of an economy still finding its way, there was a sense of new possibilities and Erastus was determined to be part of them. He knew he could do more with the mill site than grind his neighbor's corn, as throughout Connecticut new enterprises were developing along its many rivers and streams using the power of the water to manufacture products demanded by the growing nation. What was holding him back was his grandfather's reluctance to allow any change at the mill and Erastus nodded to the frustrations of his father.

As earlier noted, Erastus would not have had long to wait. When his grandfather died that June, property that would have gone to his father passed to him and his brothers. It's here that the picture gets a bit fuzzy as the land records do not record exactly when or how the bulk of the family share went to Erastus. What is clear however is that Erastus soon emerged as the sole owner of the property that would become the Dudley Farm and the mill site. This transition took place before the 1820 census and my guess is it happened rather quickly. As mentioned earlier, Erastus's two younger brothers, Prosper and Oliver would leave North Guilford and settle elsewhere, part of the great western migration that took place throughout the 19th century. Prosper would move to Alabama and Oliver to Ohio. The case of Loveman is different. How long he remained in Guilford is unclear. There is a record of him selling a five acre tract of land in November, 1811 to his uncle Jared Dudley[3]. He then apparently resurfaces in Rockbridge County, Virginia. He married Patience Thomas in 1822 and they had twin daughters, Martha and Mary in 1823 and a son Frederic in 1825. Whether he moved to Virginia prior to his marriage is not clear and record of all five members of the family disappears in Connecticut. What is clear however is that Loveman sold close to 35 acres with a barn across from the mill lot to Erastus in 1812. Containing a barn, this lot would form the heart of the Dudley Farm and the site of the first and later second homes of Erastus.[4]

An itchiness to move on and leave the economic confines of North Guilford certainly must have played a role in the decision of the three Dudley brothers to depart. Like so many others throughout New England at the time, the American west and south seemed truly the land of milk and honey, the promised land of endless opportunities. They all knew that the land and mill site inherited from their grandfather would never be sufficient for more than one of them and with Erastus already operating the grist mill they may have seen this as an opportunity for Erastus and a chance for them to escape the bonds that had chained them all to the diminishing expectations of a small rural Connecticut community. Whether Erastus bought his brothers out is unknown but Erastus now had his opportunity and for the first time his future was in his own hands.

The first house that Erastus built no longer stands on the Dudley Farm and its exact location was mostly a topic of conjecture during the early years of Fire Company's tenure. Oral tradition passed down to David from his father had placed the location roughly in the southwest corner of the property within or near a grove of trees not far from the Durham Road. David had relayed the story of how the house was moved north to its present location on the right side of the Durham Road just south of the intersection with County Road approximately ¼ mile from the present Dudley Farm property. According to David, the house had been moved for two days through the fields that existed at the time between the two sites to the east of the road by teams of oxen. It must have been a tortuously slow and difficult route to take since the land to this day is not only hilly but crossed by the Menunkatuck River. A comparison of maps in the Guilford Free Library shows the house on the property in 1856 as that of Erastus's son Ebenezer and not on the site in 1864. It is interesting to speculate on why the route across the fields was chosen, perhaps a toll would have been charged but more than likely the existing bridge across the river would not have accommodated the size and weight of the house.

I had the opportunity to conduct a series of archeological excavations on what turned out to be the site of the house beginning in the spring of 1994 as part of the Dudley Farm class and a summer school program. The first task was to test the area for possible archeological evidence that would correspond with a former dwelling. A series of test pits soon revealed that it was in fact located on the edge of what was then a meadow just to the north of the grove of trees. Working within the confines of that area, we were soon able to establish the exact location of the structure and using measurements from the house as it still stands today, were able to determine through our excavations not only the location of windows and doors, but the alignment of the house to the road. As we slowly excavated a series of one meter by one meter measured squares by scraping away the soil slowly and evenly with hand trowels, the trenches dug to remove even the foundation stones, back filled with a darker dirt, became evident and were a testimony to the recycling inclinations of the time.

Artifacts found on the site after sifting through the dirt removed from the squares were from the late 18th through mid-19th centuries corresponding to the time when the home would have been occupied by Erastus and his family and later, his son Ebenezer. They included numerous pottery shards from that time period as well as other forms of domestic debris such as pieces of beef, pork, and sheep bones that were part of their meals, clam shells, nails, and other items which were typical of a family of modest means and were a good indicator of the relative wealth of those who lived in the home. From the scatter of the artifacts it was even possible to locate a side door and a front entrance as well as the location of some of the windows since domestic debris was customarily thrown out of doors or windows in a scattering fashion as a form of disposal. The location of the house also lent further evidence that the foundation to a barn that had come down in the 1960's and is now the site of the Munger Barn on the property, was the original 18th century barn on the farm. Located close to the barn site is the original well now capped by a large stone.

One of the more interesting, and for me special artifacts found from within the area that would have been inside the house was a small metal anchor approximately four inches in length and width. Over the years I came to speculate on its purpose which was more than likely very utilitarian. But in my imagination the anchor became a keepsake and memorial to the lost oldest brother who had died at sea. I wondered was it Mary who often held it in her hands as she spent the later years of her life? Did she find comfort through the symbolic connection with her lost son and thus to a happier time and had Erastus kept it as a remembrance following his mother's death? With the death of her husband, it had been arranged that Mary be allowed to stay in one of the rooms in the home she had shared with Luther those many years which was often customary for widows. However, Luther had died penniless and in debt and his sons had been given the responsibility of settling his accounts through the sale of his land. Since Jared still owned the house, Mary was at least secured a home. According to the *Guilford Probate Records*, she was also allotted a table, chair and bed.

Back at the Dudley Farm in the fall of 1994, financial woes and the subsequent wrangling that went with it continued. Another open house was being planned, more donations of household and farm equipment were steadily arriving, but without some sort of financial solution, the experiment that was the Dudley Farm would soon be in jeopardy. It was announced by Don Homer there was $2.00 in the farm's check book at the weekly meeting of what was now being called the board of directors. The groans and exclamations were deafening. Then as a godsend, Doug announced dramatically that a loan of $25,000.00 was to be given to the farm by the Guilford Preservation Alliance. The GPA had been formed in 1980 with the expressed mission to "preserve and protect the built and natural heritage of the town of Guilford". They had been active since their inception in saving many of Guilford's historic homes and played an active role in protecting the historic fabric of the community. By making contact with this important nonprofit organization, Doug had managed to secure the farm's future, or at least buy some time. The enthusiastic support of the Alliance and the assurance it provided us was incalculable. The gift gave the Dudley Farm for the first time a level of acceptance and legitimacy needed to assure us that we were on the right path and that the very people who saw themselves as the defenders of the town's cultural heritage thought as much. Like Erastus, we now had our opportunity and the farm's future was more securely in our hands.

Interlude Number Five

(The following essay appeared in the Curator's Corner section of the Dudley Farm Newsletter, Farm News, Spring of 2001. In it I wrote about the challenges involved in making changes to the farm while trying to be true to the historic fabric of what existed).

When faced with the task of saving a treasure from the past such as the Dudley Farm, many questions are asked, hard choices pondered, and difficult decisions are made. How can we best save what exists while being true to the spirit or essence of a structure, room, or piece of furniture? How can we best show what life was like on the farm around the year 1900 while maintaining that quality that makes the Dudley Farm so special?

Longtime members know that the journey of preserving and restoring the Dudley Farm began in 1991. What was left to the North Guilford Volunteer Fire Company was an old, dirty, empty and rundown farmstead last "updated" in the 1930's and 40's. It was a time capsule, but of when? The house and barns contained elements that dated back to the mid-19th Century, and like all living structures, had grown and evolved and changed over 150 years. The questions began—what to be saved? What could be saved? What to replace? How?

The Dudley Farm you visit this spring and summer is a much different place than the day the Fire Company took possession. Over the past nine years much has changed yet much has stayed the same. Where possible, what existed that could be saved has been preserved. What needed to be restored or replaced has. Yet the process is ongoing and will be for the life of the Dudley Farm as a museum. What we have attempted to do is bring the house and property back by being true to what elements and clues still exist, to what they might have looked like in the year 1900. The truth is, we will never know. But, as we collectively learn about what homes and farms were like, we have been able to make choices.

Some may suggest that preservation means keeping only what existed, in not allowing for an element to be altered or replaced. If that is the case, then what about the leaking roof, rotten sill, or dangerously cracked plaster on the ceiling? What we have been able to do at the Dudley Farm is preserve the spirit of the house and grounds while making choices necessary to accurately and safely represent life 100 years ago. With patched walls newly painted and papered, preserved wood work and floors, one can now enter into the elegant and genteel world of the late Victorian Era. With period gardens and ongoing work on the barns and outbuildings, it is now possible for visitors to escape to our simpler rural past. In the process, we feel we are on the right track to preserving the Dudley Farm for future generations.

In his essay, "The Same Ax, Twice" that appeared in the April 2000 edition of *Yankee Magazine*, Howard Mansfield addressed the issue of how items evolve over time. Mansfield describes how with many human creations used over time, whether a tool such as an ax or an old house, it is the life of the object over time that is important and not any changes that may have taken place. When one picks up an old ax with a new handle or when a new roof replaces one worn on a house, there is a connection with the long ago craftsman who made the first one, and to all those who have since used them. In doing so, we commit ourselves to the continuing vision that created and carried the life of the original.

As a living, evolving organization, the Dudley Foundation is excited about what has been accomplished over the past few months and nine years. We are also eager to continue growing in our knowledge of the past and the promise of the future.

Chapter Six

Great Expectations

*A thing long expected takes the form
of the unexpected when at last it comes.*
—MARK TWAIN

Tom and I could not believe our good fortune. Our daily assignment to work with students at the Dudley Farm was as exciting as it gets in education. What made it fun for us was the fact that we both came to the task from a different discipline, Tom as a skilled craftsman and wood shop teacher, and I as a history teacher and archeologist. We were creating something new the spring and fall semesters back in 1994 and it was exciting and challenging for us and our students. Before the word interdisciplinary had entered the vocabulary of our school district we were doing it. Tom and I had the luxury of hand picking the first group of students that spring and between us we had recruited kids who expressed an interest in independent learning and adventure, while understanding that we were going to ask them to do things regular high school students could not even dream of. We also had high academic expectations. They'd be doing rigorous primary research and producing examples of their learning that were different than anything any of them had experienced. The mix was dynamic and interesting—Ivy League bound scholars and kids for who shop had made it possible to survive in the increasingly college oriented educational system. We also wanted a mix of males and females—this was not going to be a boy only experience. They signed on game and eager.

Principal Barbara Truex had worked a minor miracle in freeing us to take the students to the farm for what was then a block of 84 minutes or two class periods. She was as committed as we were to seeing how this experiment would work. Logistically the students would have to leave the school and drive to the farm to complete their school day as would Tom and I. Since the farm was only about eight minutes away from the high school, the trip to it was not viewed as an issue. The problem of liability was, however, for both the student drive and while they were at the farm. Barbara convinced the school district it was worth covering the risk involved. News of what we doing quickly spread throughout Guilford and Tom and I later found out that the fact that the kids were heading to the farm not only to learn, but to help in its restoration and preservation was pivotal to the community rallying to support the farm. What town would not want to see their kids having such a challenging and important educational opportunity?

We had pulled together a rough outline of what we wanted the students to learn those two semesters and Tom and I drew deeply on our experience in teaching in our disciplines and got to work. We quickly learned to feed off of each other's thoughts and ideas and bring things to a place that would be meaningful not only to the students but helpful to the farm's efforts as well. After all, we reminded each other gleefully, where else could you bring kids to not only learn about 19th century life, but experience it?

Our first course of action that February on the farm was securing a place where the students could actually gather and work. The logical place was the dining room of the house, a space that was large enough for us all to gather and would allow us to at least get out of the weather. With no central heat or heat of any kind for that matter, the students soon learned those first two months the meaning of what it was like to be cold. It did not take them long to grasp the 19th century practice of layering. Then it snowed. As those of us in Connecticut know, those last two months of winter can be cruel weather-wise and our intrepid students did their best to understand that snow was more than just an inconvenience, but a factor that added another whole layer of challenges to life on a farm 100 years ago. They became experts on predicting the weather, and soon were able to read the clouds, wind direction, and other signs those in the past would have used on a daily basis to understand what nature had in store for them.

The first challenge they faced was learning about the farm, how those who lived there 100 years ago would have used each room in the house, each outbuilding, and the big barn that dominated just to the right of the house. Then we put them to work. Due to the weather, the first area of focus was the house itself. By studying the exterior, students were able to understand the development and evolution of the styles blended into the home over the 150 years since it was built and the challenges inherent to its restoration and preservation. In the interior, they learned about the use of space 100 years ago and what the cultural meanings were inherent in that use. With Doug, Henry, and Bob from the board of directors, Tom and I worked out a list of what we could realistically have the students do to help in the restoration. The first task was cleaning the many rooms of the accumulated dirt and dust of the past thirty years and to have them pick through and accurately identify and catalogue what items remained in the house, no matter how small or seemingly insignificant.

At this point it might be best to let a number of the students speak for themselves. One of the things Tom and I insisted on was that they each kept a journal of their thoughts and experiences. Some of them were shared in what was an early version of the *Farm News* then put together by Doug. This first entry was written by students Bryan Johnson and Alex Effgen. In it they described their first day at the farm:

> … we decided to write about the first day we went to the Dudley Farm. Our very first impression of the farm can be summed up in two adjectives, cold and slippery. The first time our feet touched Dudley soil we slipped on the icy terrain and all but cracked our heads. But after the dangerous trek to the front steps (crawling), we went inside.

Bryan and Alex then described their impression of the house:

> Once in the actual premises the place was in a state of disarray, but structurally it was intact. The wallpaper was peeling, all four different layers of them. Dust covered the floor, along with scattered garbage. To sum things up, it was a dump (pardon our language). Then after viewing the first floor, we went to the

second floor. We'd say it was in better condition than the first (but not by much). In a few of the rooms there were boxes full of bills and letters and photographs that belonged to the Dudley's of the olden days.

They then took us outside for their first impressions there:

Next we left the house and analyzed the surroundings. We'd say that the many types of barns that were there in the area were in a lot better condition than the house but we would be lying. In actuality, some of the barns were basically being held together by a thread (or in this case a splinter). In one room of the main barn there was actually bat guano as far as the eye could see. Luckily there was a clean room for us to work in. (That is, it was clean after we took all of the artifacts out of it).

Bryan and Alex closed with an editorial statement:

Now all this information and editorialization may seem negative about the Dudley Farm, but this is an article about our first day impressions. The both of us have hope and great expectations towards the positive benefits that the renovated Dudley Farm will give to the town of Guilford. It is groups like ours and people like the ones that give their time and effort to the renovation that will help show how the nineteenth century life used to be led. God bless America!

Student Jonathan Leake also reflected on his first day at the farm in his journal. Jonathan wrote that his first day on the farm:

...was quite an experience. It was a cold day, but very sunny outside. It was probably the first day that was not snowed out or given a delay to school for a month. When we all arrived one of the first comments was "what a dump". Then Mr. Powers told us to look at the positive side to this farm and all the strong points to it.

Jon Hunt wrote:

> On the first day that I visited the Dudley Farm I had many
> mixed reactions. First the house was very large. I had expected
> it to be much smaller because it was built so long ago... The
> many rooms in the house were empty except for the cobwebs
> and dirt. The whole house had a very distinct smell to it. The
> wallpaper and paint are peeling on the inside and the paint on
> the outside.

Jon then wrote about what he saw of the outbuildings and barn:

> ...we went to the many barns on the property. The sugar shack
> in the back of the property is in ruins. It would be impossible
> to fix it, you would have to take the whole place down and start
> over. The other small barns are also in pretty bad condition.
> The big barn in front has many different sections to it. In the
> back of the barn there is a room that we call the bat room. In
> the early spring thousands of bats come and live in the barn.
> Many people would like the bats exterminated. That should
> definitely not be done. If they want that done then a special
> barn should be built for the sole use of the bats. The main part
> of the barn is in good condition, it just needs to be cleaned up
> a little bit...[1]

This was the farm the students saw, a rather naive but enthusiastic look,
that was in reality an honest view of the condition of the farm, house
and outbuildings that late winter of 1994. Their descriptions encapsulate the magnitude of the job that faced the Dudley Farm organization.
In so many ways the enormous extent of the project would have dis-
suaded anyone with experience in such matters as restoring and creating a property that included all it did into a museum. The irony of it all
was that the board of directors of the farm really had no idea—just a
determination born of a tradition that reached across generations, and
in the end, that was the secret to their success.

The grist mill and dam site on which Erastus would focus his future hopes was, by the standard of the day, not one with a tremendous amount of potential. The relatively meager flow of water provided by the Menunkatuck River (today known as the West River) was usually sufficient for a small grist mill operation such as the one he had inherited from his grandfather. For something more, changes would have had to be made. In our more technologically developed world, it is easy to forget the importance of water at a time when it was the primary and most important source of mechanical power. Since ancient times, people had harnessed the force of falling or swiftly moving water to turn water wheels that would provide the energy to grind grain into flour or propel simple machines. By 1812, Americans, especially here in New England, were beginning to tap that power to begin the process of industrialization first begun a half century earlier in Great Britain. The grist mill that the Dudley family had operated was an example of the more ancient technology. Erastus, it is clear, was contemplating something more. His first priority would have to be to secure enough water to provide the force needed to do more than just turn a mill stone.

A visit to the mill site today reveals what can best be described as the ruins of the dam and the jumbled foundations of all that Erastus built. Owned by the town of Guilford since the mid-20th century, it has been ravaged by floods that have struck the region during that century. The hurricanes of 1938 and 1955 did tremendous damage. The great flood of 1982, when small long neglected dams such as this burst under the pressure of unrelenting rains, finished off what time and the other storms had left undone. Many of the great stones used in the structure of the dam and attendant raceways designed to channel water to wheels have been thrown about and tossed downstream, testimony to the power of water. The site has since continued to erode as each storm sends water through what is left, slowly chiseling away what the Dudley's had built.

But if one looks beyond the scatter of stones and overgrown brush that marks the site, enough still remains to get an idea of what was once there. The remnant of the dam is there, the silted mill pond, the broken stone foundations, and eroded channels through which the water still runs on its way to Long Island Sound all speak of a time when Erastus Dudley was able to turn his dream into reality.

The dam is still the most prominent component of the mill site and what remains was clearly built in the style of the early 19th century. Though much of it has been destroyed, the main section which was capped by a spillway that formed the bulk of the structure still exists. This part of the dam was designed to hold back the water and form the mill pond behind it. The spillway was created to allow excess water to flow from the dam and thus relieve any pressure building up during storms or other times of high water. Today the dam to the casual observer looks like an elongated pile of stones but that's purely on the surface. Underneath is a structure that represented the cutting edge of hydraulic technology at the time it was built. It is certainly at least the second dam on the site. The first would have been more than likely a wooden structure common during the late 17th and early 18th centuries, the first dam would certainly have needed to be replaced as the later century progressed. There is structural evidence that it may have been approximately 80 feet south of the present dam and in all likelihood was that of Jared and Luther Dudley. The stone remains of what is apparently the original gristmill are located there. The existing dam is a new structure erected during the time of Erastus based on the design and remains of surrounding buildings. There is also a possibility that it is a composite structure added to and changed over time.

Dams like that of the Dudley's were engineered to last and it is a testimony to the building skill of those who built it that it has survived all these years despite a lack of even minimal maintenance over the past century. Its construction would have taken place during August, normally the driest month of the year and thus the time of lowest water in the river. The dam itself would have been built in two separate identical sections, each anchored to either bank, the end to the west attached to the rock ledge and that to the east to the gently sloping hill that led up to the Durham Road. Construction of the first section would have begun as soon as a coffer, or temporary dam, was built to divert the flow of the river away from the area and over to the side where the other section was to be built. These coffers were usually a series of wooden boxes lined end to end and filled with stones, with clay often stacked between them to form a seal. Once the coffer was in place work could begin on the construction of the dam.

The first task was to clear the bed where the dam was to be built of rubble. Trenches were then dug in which the bottom of a wooden frame would be placed. The frame, made of timbers and joined together with a mortise and tenon system using wooden pegs much as a house or barn frame would have, was then erected. This frame formed the basic shape of the dam which was a ramp, usually six feet high on the front end and sloping twenty five feet or so down to the stream bed on the back side. This appears to be roughly the size of the Dudley dam. The frame was then filled with stones, with the front face constructed as a foundation would with dry-laid stones carefully fit into place to form a wall like structure. Behind that stone face the frame was filled with rocks and rubble of varying sizes packed in to form the massive bulk of the dam. The long slope of the ramp was then usually capped or lined with a layer of boards creating a smooth surface for the water to flow up, against, and over the dam. Across the top edge of the dam a cap log was usually constructed to reduce the wear on that section as the water flowed over it. The combined weight of the stones and rubble fill, along with the water, would hold the dam in place. After the first section of the dam was completed, the coffer dam was removed and reconstructed to divert the water to the other side while the second part was built. Once completed, the dam would have held back the water of the Mennunkatuck River creating the mill pond.

The mill pond was the key to the entire site. The water it held would provide the power for the water wheel that would turn the mill stones in the case of the grist mill. The next task was construction of the stone lined channels designed to allow the water to flow to the wheel. The Dudley site appears to have had two of these, one for the grist mill and the other for a number of different mill operations created by Erastus between the years 1820 and 1850. Each of these channels, called raceways, would have been around four to six feet wide and around six feet deep. The section built into the dam to allow water to flow from the mill pond to the mill was called a head race and would have had a wooden gate that could be raised up to allow water to flow into the race and lowered to shut the water off. In this way water would only be used when needed. The race would then continue either underneath the mill, which was the case of the gristmill, or to the side of it which was the case of the other mill buildings. There the water would encounter the great wheel which would be turned by the velocity of the flow of water as it ran through the race. Once the water passed the wheel it would exit through the end of the raceway and back to the river. This last section was called a tail race.

It was the end of August and Erastus stood on the dam just outside the mill and surveyed the millpond with a knowing eye. Water is low, he thought, and unless some storms came soon to raise the level he might not have enough to mill the corn and wheat his neighbors would soon be bringing. At least with the corn he had some time as they would need to dry the kernels. But on the positive side, the dry weather would allow him time to make repairs on the wheel and drive train. Many of the paddles on the wheel were beginning to show their age and his job today was to begin to replace them. His thoughts drifted fondly back to the days when as a boy, his father had shown him how it was done, patiently putting up with his bungling attempts to do the hard work that was a millwrights lot. She needs constant care his father would say of the wheel. "Boy," he'd say, "she is like a good woman, her happiness runs with the attention you give her". They'd both laugh and get back to the task. How many of these had he since replaced?

The wheel and gearing of a mill powered by water needed constant maintenance as most parts during the early 1800's were still made of wood and would wear out and break from the pressure exerted by the water and use. Like most millwrights, as a person who was skilled in the construction and running these delicate mechanical devices were called, Erastus would have been skilled at their maintenance and repair. A mill unable to run when needed was a potential economic catastrophe not only for its owner but all those that depended upon its services.

The location of the gristmill is today on what can be best described as a small and quickly eroding island in the middle of the river. It is held together by the roots of small trees that have overgrown it but the remnant of the raceway that ran directly underneath the building is still clearly visible. Standing on the island and facing north towards the dam, the gristmill site is separated from both river banks by the remains of the second raceway to the east towards the Durham Road and the river as it flows over the spillway of the dam to the west. According to Oliver Evans, who wrote the *The Young Mill-Wright and Miller's Guide*, first published during the early 19th century as the "how to" book of its time on the subject, it is possible to actually estimate what size and type the Dudley wheel that powered the mill would have been.

Evans describes how all water wheels utilized what he termed the "fall" of water, which was literally the distance the water falls from the height of the dam to the point where it strikes the paddles on the wheel. The fall provides the speed and force of the water necessary to turn the wheel. Because the height of the dam was never greater than 8 feet, the charts Evans provides indicate that in all likelihood the Dudley's utilized a type of vertical wheel called an undershot wheel. An undershot wheel provides plenty of power with relatively little fall as the water flows under the bottom of the wheel striking the paddles and turning the wheel. Based on Evans's calculations, a mill site with a fall of 8 feet would require an undershot wheel 12 feet in diameter, which would revolve 24 times per minute, and turn a four foot wide mill stone 106 times per minute. The wheel would have been as wide as the stone it turned, in this case four feet, and the shaft the wheel turned to provide power to the gearing that turned the stone would have been 24 to 26 inches in diameter.[2] The wheel would have been placed in what was called the wheel pit under the mill building, allowing for the fall of water the eight feet from the head race.

Because the gristmill was literally in front of the dam, approximately 35 feet from the eastern end, one would have had to cross over that section of the dam to reach it. That part of the dam would thus have been built up and widened enough for a wagon to cross from the river bank to the building in order to load and unload safely. The exact size of the mill itself due to the scant remains caused by erosion and the fact that oral tradition tells of the Dudley's actually dismantling and recycling materials from all the buildings on the site, is difficult if impossible to determine. Typically a gristmill of its size might have been a one story building approximately 30 by 30 square feet.

In the 1820 Census, Erastus Dudley is listed as a farmer. Having acquired enough land from his grandfather to support his family, around 250 acres that included the present Dudley Farm, undoubtedly that was his main focus. The gristmill, operated seasonally based on demand, would not have provided enough work or income for him to support his quickly growing family. In 1820 Erastus and Ruth had eight children ranging in age from one to13 including two sets of twins and they would add two more within three years. We can only imagine the pressure mounting on him to provide for them all and during the new decade Dudley appears to have turned his attention to the mill site and in the process of transforming it he transformed his family's future as well.

Dudley also was part owner of a saw mill located further downstream, the old Captain Ward's mill in North Guilford and a carding mill as well. These both would have provided him with some capital that along with the gristmill and would be crucial to his later transformation of the gristmill site. Ironically, both the other two mills he had ownership in represented both the past and future of North Guilford and the region in general. From its very beginning as a settlement, Guilford, and later North Guilford relied heavily on timber as a main source of income. High demand for it in England and Europe made it possible for many Connecticut and New England towns to prosper throughout the Colonial Era. There is even record of pre-built houses being dismantled and shipped to the Caribbean colonies. Abundant timber also supplied the many shipyards that sprang up throughout the region, including at least three in Guilford and was the primary cash crop and the economic engine of its day.

But by 1820 that was all coming quickly to an end. Close to two hundred years of timbering had denuded the landscape and that, along with the demand for fire wood, had put a serious strain on the resource. At a time when the average home in Connecticut consumed up to thirty cords of wood a year for cooking and heat in inefficient fireplaces, what was left of the woods were jealously husbanded as woodlots by those who had them. The saw mill, once a boon to its owners, probably existed more as a source for local farmers and others to have their timbers sawed into boards and planks as they needed them. Sawmills, like gristmills, also usually serviced an area of roughly eight square miles due to the difficulty in hauling heavy loads over greater distances. Therefore this mill, like the one that ground grain, would have fallen into operating on an on demand basis.

The carding mill is a different story. By 1820 the boom industry throughout New England was wool. Woolen textile mills were being built throughout the region and located where there was enough water power to power sometimes hundreds of mechanical looms. Seemingly overnight the landscape of New England was being transformed. The Industrial Revolution had arrived and mill towns sprang up where ever there was enough water to turn the great wheels. Willimantic, Torrington, Rockville and other industrial towns sprang up seemingly overnight along their fast moving larger streams and falls. The economy of the region would never be the same. Guilford however, located on the coastal plain, did not have the type of rivers and streams needed to become an industrial center. Its development in that area stayed small in scale and limited. But it did have the land, now mostly pasture with the disappearance of the forest, perfect for raising the resource these new textile mills craved: wool.

Sheep began to appear in and around Guilford in large numbers by 1820 as farmers realized the profits they could make from this new and growing industry. Traditionally, local farmers like the rest of their New England brethren, had kept a number of sheep for the production of wool for their family's use. The wool, hand carded and then spun at home by the women of the family into thread, would have then been transformed into clothing for their use or sold to traveling merchants who gathered it to be sold in larger urban markets. But as the demand for wool skyrocketed and the number of sheep dotting the hills of North Guilford multiplied, a carding mill became essential to the livelihood of local farmers. A carding mill utilized a water driven spiked roller that cleaned and stretched the raw wool fibers into long fluffy units called bats that would then be transported in bulk to a woolen mill to be spun into thread and eventually woven into cloth. This proved key for Erastus Dudley and his plans for his own mill site. Exactly who his partners in this mill has not yet been determined but for the purposes of the Dudley Farm's story, it appears that the carding mill may have provided him with an influx of capital that allowed him to put his plans into motion.

His plan to rebuild the dam and construct a second raceway was well underway. Erastus had hired laborers from Guilford town to help in the work, strong men who were hungry for the work being landless and some even transient. The key was to keep their desire for spirits at bay while they toiled. He was also pleased with the engineer he had hired, a man who had a strong reputation and a long list of recommendations for the work he had done in building the dams and raceways for many of the new enterprises being built in the eastern part of the state. In two more weeks Erastus hoped to see the work done as his budget would allow no longer.

With the opening of the new Pautapaug (Essex) and Fair Haven Turnpike, the possibilities for his mill site promised to increase. The traffic moving through his land on the new macadamized road would potentially make his plan to build a bone mill on the site pay off in large dividends. Once that second raceway was built and the dam rebuilt to store more water, the bone mill would provide a new and potentially lucrative source of income. His plan was not to manufacture implements of bone as many elsewhere were but to provide the bone plugs and strips they could then shape and cut into items such as buttons, handles, and combs. He would be a supplier of the materials they need. Local farmers were enthused about his scheme; he'd be offering them another source of income for the cattle they raised. He'd also grind the pieces he could not offer to manufacturers into a powdery meal that was growing in popularity as something new called fertilizer for farmers' fields. So in effect he could sell back to them what he had initially purchased, making a profit in the process.

As Erastus watched the work of fitting the large stones that lined the raceway into place, he was pleased with what he knew was a promising beginning. His dreams were becoming a reality and he now had great expectations for the future. After all, it was 1828 and the turmoil and economic problems of past years were gone. There was a new national confidence born of new circumstances and Erastus could not help but feel himself part of it. "Yes", he said to himself as he watched a heavy wagon driven by its attentive teamster cross the bridge built over the river south of his mill on the new turnpike, "things are different now, I do have great expectations". He smiled as he walked over to inspect the progress of the stone masons as they jostled another stone into place.

Interlude Number Six

(The following was written by Jim Smith, a senior at Guilford High School during the spring semester of 1994 and a member of the first Dudley Farm class. In his journal entry he writes about the possibilities…)

Why the Dudley Farm is Important

The Dudley Farm is a very useful resource for our future. Both students and the general public all across Connecticut can learn about New England's past and maybe even a bit about its future. Although the Dudley Farm is not in the best condition it is a gold mine for learning. Because of the well preserved structures still standing we are able to see firsthand many of the different styles of architecture from the past 200 years. David Dudley has left us with a surplus of information about the past and the opportunity to create a living, breathing, textbook. With proper restoration the Dudley property will be transformed into a functioning old New England farm environment…

The North Guilford Volunteer Fire Department and Guilford High School have begun some of the much needed restoration work on the old farm house. In our future the Dudley Farm will with any luck become a place for everyone to benefit from. If plans go well a living 19th century farm will be created. For students at Guilford High School the Dudley Farm Project has already been a huge success. Working with teachers, the students learn about how life was led in early Guilford through written and research projects and hands-on tasks, done as they would have been before technology took over. The Dudley Farm will be a living encyclopedia of knowledge.

Possibilities for the future of the farm are unbelievable. The hands-on experience at the farm will be a new and exciting way for students to learn. The future of the farm will benefit our society greatly in an educational and moral fashion. With proper help and funding we will have a classroom for science, social studies, and industrial arts. Guilford is very fortunate to have such a resource.[3]

Chapter Seven
The Reality of Expectations

The difference between perseverance and obstinacy is that one comes from a strong will, and the other from a strong won't.
— Henry Ward Beecher

Henry Ward Beecher was one of the most important ministers and preachers of the 19th century. Known for his passionate and fiery oratory on behalf of abolition, women's suffrage, and other causes, Beecher embodied the passionate will and powerful changes that typified the age in which he lived. Born in Litchfield, Connecticut in 1813, Beecher was a contemporary of Erastus Dudley and his sons. He was the son of Rev. Lyman Beecher, arguably one of the most remarkable men of his generation and an intellectual force who helped shape the nation's moral struggle against slavery. Henry was also brother of Harriet Beecher Stowe whose novel, *Uncle Tom's Cabin*, was famously credited with helping to start the Civil War by President Abraham Lincoln.

Beecher's mother was Roxanna Foote, born and raised in Guilford. There she met her husband Lyman as he would spend time when on breaks from his studies at Yale with his aunt Catherine (Lyman) Benton and her husband Lot who had adopted him. It was said of Roxanna that she was a woman of "remarkable intellectual powers, great personal attractions, and a most gentle, lovely, and engaging temper".[1] Her influence on her eleven children was instrumental in motivating them to become agents of positive change. Harriet often stated how, as children, she and her siblings spent much time in Guilford. Perhaps those times helped shape the qualities of character they would all become famous for. The Beecher family epitomized the 19th century belief that each person must take action to create a better world, a concept that Erastus Dudley would certainly have understood and embraced. Although there is no evidence that they ever met, it's not hard to imagine the Beechers, traveling north along the Durham Road as they journeyed back to Litchfield, passing the Dudley mill and noticing the activity there as Erastus began the process of rebuilding the dam and mill buildings during the 1820's and 30's.

Perseverance was definitely a quality of character that Erastus Dudley had to possess. He may have been a bit obstinate as well simply because once committed to his transformation of the Dudley mill site he was most likely unwilling to accept not succeeding. In many ways both words, perseverance and obstinacy, also encapsulate the Dudley Farm board of directors as the 1990's evolved. Through bouts of both, they were able to take what Erastus had created as a legacy for his family that extended well into the 20th century, embrace that legacy, and bring it into the 21st.

For the Dudley Farm, things truly began to move forward as 1995 unfolded into 1996. A new vitality and sense of purpose had come with the loan from the Guilford Preservation Alliance and renewed commitment by Guilford High School to run the Dudley Farm class. For the first time a concerted effort was made to fundraise and appeal to the community for membership in the Dudley Foundation. Funds were allocated for the creation of a brochure that could be mailed and distributed throughout Guilford and the entire effort was headed up by George Curry who generously volunteered to take on the co-ordination of this arduous task. The State of Connecticut officially designated the Dudley Foundation as a legally established non-profit entity to oversee and manage the farm in 1995, and Buster Scranton became the first president when the board of directors was officially elected at the foundation's first annual meeting that October. The first board was made up of those who had overseen those bleak days in 1994; Bob Ashman, Henry Tichy, Joan Stettbacher, Don Homer, Charlie Hammarlund, Doug Williamson, Tom Leddy, and me. Six of the nine board members, including Buster as president, were from the Fire Company as designated in the new Foundation's by-laws.

Work proceeded on the house in particular that spring and summer as volunteers painted the outside a gleaming white. For the first time in many years the Dudley house could again stand proudly on the hill overlooking the Durham Road, refreshed and renewed. Bob and Henry in particular dismantled and repaired most of the windows and took on the time consuming task of scraping, repairing, and repainting the green shutters that had so long graced the exterior. By that fall the house became a true beacon of change and growth, testimony to the persistent efforts of those dedicated to saving it.

The Dudley Farm class was in full swing with the number of students increased to fifteen each semester. Most of the students were seniors and committed to take the course for a full year. This allowed Tom and me to implement our newly designed curriculum while giving the students an opportunity to allow both their academic and hands-on skills to grow. The course would focus on five main areas of study, all integrated and ongoing throughout the year. Each area of study included research, application, and hands-on experiences designed to give students a chance to immerse themselves in the life of the farm the Dudley's had created. The areas of study were:

1. Genealogical and historical research on the Dudley family.
2. The study, preservation, and restoration of the Dudley house and outbuildings.
3. The study of farm organization, work, and building usage.
4. The study of the Dudley Mills.
5. The study of daily life in the 19th century.

The class was a joy to teach for Tom and I and we were constantly amazed at the enthusiasm and dedication the students exhibited on a routine basis. Not only were they researching, practicing, and applying their new found knowledge of the past, students became passionately committed to their experience and the idea of helping to save the farm. The hands-on aspect; whether working to repair a building, constructing a fence, making butter, or learning to spin wool into yarn, allowed the students through their hourly immersion in 19th century life to become connected to the past in a way no other history course could. They could see every day that what they were doing mattered and their sense of pride in that was a wonder to see. It was contagious.

With Tom's attentive patience, the students that year tackled their first major restoration project, rebuilding and replacing the sills on the post and beam shed directly behind the house. This building had been used for a variety of purposes during its life, most recently over the past forty years as a catch-all storage area. Among the piles of broken and discarded items, all of which the students tried to identify if possible and catalogue, were mounds of rags and discarded parts of rag rugs. It soon became obvious that one of the various "home industries" that took place on the farm was the production of these rugs. Talks with older residents in the area soon confirmed that around the turn of the last century rag rug production had become a cottage industry in North Guilford and that many of the old looms long not used for the production of fabric were converted to that purpose. It was not long before the Potter family of North Guilford donated a large wooden loom used for that purpose and it was repaired and eventually set up in the house to demonstrate rag rug making.

While the students were learning the fine art of timber framing in their work on the shed, volunteers led once again by Henry and Bob replaced the earthen floor with concrete. The goal was to convert the space into a workshop area that could be used by the students and the farm volunteers and soon the old shed had a new life. It turned out that one of the fascinating aspects of the building was that among its many purposes in the past was the fact that under the southwest corner was a storage cistern for water. An elaborate gutter system drained water from the roof of the house to the basin for use in the house as a water supply. This supplemented the well and another larger cistern under the windmill located between the house and the main barn that was actually filled by the windmill as it pumped water from the Menunkatuck River across the Durham Road. That cistern then gravity fed water to the main barn. With Doug's help in figuring out how the system actually worked, students were able to study how an intricate system of utilizing gravity and a wind driven pump guaranteed the Dudley's all the water they and their animals might need.

While work was being done on the shed, students continued their study of 19th century life with frequent trips to the Guilford Town Hall to research the history of the Dudley family and the property by searching through the Guilford Land and Probate Records. They soon became as skilled as any attorney at deciphering the sometimes close to illegible hand written documents, some dating to the late 17th century. This task would continue over the next few years and proved invaluable in helping to understand and document the history of the Dudley's farm and family.

Work continued on the interior of the house also as peeling and torn wall paper was removed, samples saved, and the task of patching plaster walls was begun. Together with farm volunteers, the slow process of transforming the interior of the house to the circa 1900 time period was becoming a reality. Attention was turned to the property as well and with a site survey created earlier by Doug; students were able to establish the use of many of the outbuildings. Because many of them were beyond repair, this task was crucial in documenting their existence. That year the farm began to move forward with a plan to understand the past use of the land and develop its use in the future. One plan was to establish the practice of organic gardening.

Among interested local and now Foundation members were a group of organic gardeners and part time farmers. As members of the Northeast Organic Farmers Association, they were committed to helping to transform the region's food supply into organic and local. They leapt at the opportunity to start an organic garden on the farm and what became known as the Lower field was chosen as the logical site. This site eventually evolved into the Dudley Farm's highly successful Community Garden in later years. Work also began on the documentation and restoration of the flower and herb gardens that once graced the farm which had always been locally noted and admired, especially under David's grandmother Martha and mother Amy. The herb garden eventually became a labor of love for Bill and Peggy Barnes as they meticulously created and tended it those early years. Farm volunteers Jerri Guadagno and Linda Curry, among many others began the long process of reclaiming and restoring the flower gardens that had once embellished the outside of the house with color and life. Persistence was paying off. The Dudley Farm was becoming something more than a dream.

The optimism of the Dudley Foundation during the mid-1990's can best be summed up by the brochure that was created and mailed to Guilford residents in early 1996, which was the first official membership and fund raising effort under the auspices of the Dudley Foundation. An expensive effort for the farm, it was none-the-less viewed as an important next step in the establishment of the farm as a self-sustaining non-profit entity by most of the board of directors. Some legitimately questioned the size, scope, and cost of the effort and thus revealed for the first time a significant difference within the group view of what the farm in the end should be. The dynamic vision encapsulated in the brochure represented a possible growth and change that challenged the notion of the farm being a representation of the local community and its past and was also perceived as a financial recklessness that the more fiscally conservative members found dangerous.

The brochure cover contained three words that highlighted the main goals of the Foundation: Renewal, Growth, and Community. It stated:

The Dudley Farm:
A Unique and Vital
Piece of Connecticut History

The first page inside the brochure described the history of the farm and the effort of the North Guilford Volunteer Fire Company to create the Dudley Foundation in order to preserve, restore, and operate the farm as a historical, educational, and recreational resource. The next page highlighted the Foundation's mission to "serve the general public as a museum, education center, and recreation park". Each part of the mission was explained in detail with the addition of the plan to re-establish the farm as a working farm in order to best represent the past.

The brochure went on reach out to individuals, organizations, and businesses and detailed how they could help through membership and donations and how renewal and growth were only possible through the participation of the general public and that together it was possible to build the vision into a reality. It was a profound appeal and in the end an overall success. Because a brochure was mailed to every residence and business in Guilford as well as those from surrounding communities that had already expressed their interest and support, membership in the foundation began to grow and donations began to arrive. The appeal had worked and the farm's future seemed brighter than ever.

Erastus could hardly believe his good fortune. The construction of the new dam had proceeded in a timely manner and the dry, hot August weather had held. He marveled at the cyclopean stones the oxen were slowly pulling into place to form the face and top of the structure. Mostly field stones from the ledges behind his old homestead, many had also come from neighbors' land to the north, south, and east as they gladly donated them to the project. Of course, the time and cost to secure them and sled them to the site was substantial. But it had been worth it as one stone of size could replace countless smaller. The plan to take apart the dam of his grandfather, 80 feet below his new one, had saved time and secured a ready supply of material, adding to a faster pace of construction than had been anticipated. He had worried what impact that would have on his aging gristmill but had been assured that water could still be diverted to it during construction to turn the wheel. And so it had. Soon a new one would take its place. The cut stones were another matter however as they formed the footing for the new raceways and the precise fit added to the overall stability. The stone mason had found some good stones locally but many had to be dragged on oxen pulled sleds from as far away as the quarries at Stoney Creek ten miles to the southwest. Until they had been set into place the all-important race construction had lagged. But that was behind them now and soon the work could turn to his plans for the mills.

In 1830 Erastus Dudley was still listed as a farmer in the U.S. Census so the changes that took place at the mill might still have been evolving. The dam rebuilding certainly needed to proceed once begun thus that work might have taken place either just prior to or shortly after that date. Interestingly, Dudley never had himself listed as a millwright, tanner, or any other occupation associated with the mill site despite the fact that his income during the 1820's, 30's, and 40's would have depended heavily upon the activity that took place along the Menunkatuck River. The only exception was in 1850, with the tannery closed, Erastus lists himself as a merchant, an occupation that will be addressed later. By 1860 and 70 however, he is once again listed as a farmer. My sense is that throughout his life Erastus felt it important to associate himself with the traditional landed class in Guilford despite the tremendous economic changes that were increasingly making that status both quaint and insignificant. Though he obviously embraced change in order to propel his and his family's prospects into the future, his continued identification with farming and the land suggests to us his true character and values. He certainly would have identified with the quest begun by his North Guilford neighbors 170 years later.

In the census of 1830, Dudley continued to show part owner-ship in the carding and saw mills and had property listed at more than $2000.00. This included two houses with associated outbuildings including the former home of his father where he apparently resided along with his large family until moving to the small homestead he built across from the mill site on land that would become the Dudley Farm. One can only imagine how Erastus and Ruth managed to function in a small four room house with eleven children ranging in age from seven to twenty three. But circumstances were to quickly change as it is short-ly after that date that Erastus began to truly transform the mill site.

According to Bernard Steiner in his *History of Guilford and Madison, Connecticut*, Dudley was given permission by the town of Guilford in 1827 to dam the West River, then still known as the Menunkatuck, in North Guilford.[2] The expressed purpose was "for machinery". This designation meant that he was to utilize the water source to power ma-chines in a manufacturing operation. Over the next 14 years Erastus established a variety of operations and mills that used water driven equipment; the grist mill, a bone mill, a bark mill, and a tannery. These businesses were successful enough to firmly place his family on all four corners of the intersection of the Durham Road and Fair Haven Turn-pike and the area became known as Dudleyville well into the next cen-tury. Of the four enterprises, the tannery became the most important.

During the first half of the 19th century the production of leather products, especially shoes, was the largest industry in Guilford and many surrounding communities.[3] The industry blossomed during the 1820's and peaked around 1840 as tanneries were set up throughout the region to produce the processed hides necessary to support them. The Dudley tannery, the only one in North Guilford, was started by Erastus some time shortly after 1830 and operated for roughly 20 years before ceasing operation shortly after 1850. Small localized tanneries like that of the Dudley's bought hides from surrounding farmers and then sold them processed, back to members of the community who then produced the leather into shoes in small shops or at home, creating a regional cottage industry that often allowed farmers and others to supplement their income. Traveling merchants then bought the shoes to be sold throughout the region and the U.S., with many sold in the South to plantation owners for their slaves.

Although little remains of the tannery along the river now other than the broken dam and scattered foundations, it is possible to establish where steps in tanning took place. Tanning was a rather lengthy process that took a minimum of eight months and often as long as a year to produce a cured and workable piece of leather. The raw materials were rather simple and easily accessible for the Dudley's: hides from local cattle and sheep, lime, oak or hemlock bark, and water.

According to an 1841 land transaction between Erastus and four of his sons, Luther F., Erastus F., Ebenezer F., and Nathan C., the land along the river contained a tanyard, tannery, a currying mill and a bark mill all associated with the tanning of hides.[4] By then the property also included the grist mill, bone mill, a horse barn and a hog pound all packed onto the three acres of the site. It was a crowded, bustling space filled with the noise and foul odors of the many activities taking place; a far cry from the tranquilly wooded glen of today.

The tannery had four distinct operations and thus locations spread out along the river, the first being the hide cleaning and liming area. This activity took place just below the dam on the Durham Road side along the most easterly of the raceways. The raw, fresh hides were dipped in running water, scraped to remove any tissue still on them, then dipped into vats containing a mixture of water and lime repeatedly over the course of a day or two. They would then be taken from the vats and scraped again to remove the loosened hairs. The hides were then returned to the vats for two to three days, then taken out and folded into a wet pile for four to five days or more. This process of soaking and folding was repeated for two months. The location of this operation was just south of the dam in a building that appeared to be 16^{ft} x 20^{ft}. The remains of a substantial stone foundation along the raceway is still quite evident as well as an outline of foundation stones detailing the building's overall imprint.

Following the first two months, the hides were then scraped again to remove all remaining hair and again soaked for three to four days, then stacked for a week repeatedly for three months. This prepared the hides for the second step in the process, liming which entailed soaking the hides in a thick solution of lime for one week and then stacking them for another repeatedly for four months. This second step took place in the tannery building in vats specifically built for that purpose. A survey of the site reveals that this building, located along the east bank of the now broken eastern raceway about 24 feet south of building #1 (cleaning location), had two separate sections running from west to east, the first 18^{ft} x 26^{ft} to the west open to the raceway and the second, 20^{ft} x 26^{ft}, attached to the east. This larger building housed the main tanning operation on the property.

After the initial nine months of scraping, soaking, and stacking, the hides were brought to the tanyard where they were soaked in pits positioned 24^{ft} to the south of the main tannery building where they were soaked for an additional three months. The remnant of this area is clearly visible as a 16^{ft} wide, 45^{ft} long depression. This depression held the tan pits that were more than likely lined with oak planking and divided into a series of sections to hold the hides. Each pit was layered in sequence starting at the bottom: tan bark (either oak or hemlock), then a hide, then tan bark, then another hide until the pit was filled two feet from the top. The pit was then covered with a layer of old used tan bark about a foot thick, then trampled and compressed. Once filled, the pit was continuously moistened to allow the tannin from the bark to soak into the hides to give them the warm brown color of finished leather while acting as a preservative. There would also have been a pit used to store the used tan bark for later use in this area.

The final step in the production of leather took place back in the main tannery building in an area called the currying mill. Here the hides were processed and conditioned with oil or grease made from animal fat and thus made ready for the shoemakers and other craftsmen who made saddles, harnesses, and belts. There is a possibility that water power may have been used during this step to work the grease or oil continuously into the leather though whether or not the Dudley's performed this step by machine or hand is impossible to tell.

Throughout the months of turning a raw hide into finished leather, the Dudley's would have had ready access to all the resources needed. The hides and animal fat was supplied by local farmers and the bark that was ground into chip-like pieces came from local sources as well, including refuse from the saw mill that Erastus still partly owned. The lime so integral to the creation of leather was easily obtainable from the thousands of clam shells found along the local shoreline that could be gathered by the wagon-load and ground into a powder. Pieces of shells can still be found strewn about the site as well as across the road at the old homestead site. All and all the tannery proved to be quite lucrative for Erastus and by 1841 he was ready to turn over the entire operation to his sons.

In 1841, Luther Frederic Dudley was 27 years old. The second oldest son of Erastus and Ruth, he was the twin of his sister Lois Rossiter who had married Joel Benton, formerly of North Guilford in 1834 and unfortunately died in Illinois in 1838. Though twins, Luther had been born a day later than his sister. In 1840, Luther was listed in the census as a tanner and had married Eliza Buck in October, 1838. A year later the Guilford Land Records[5] show he received a house that still stands on the southeast corner of the intersection of Ct Routes 80 and 77 from his father. The document reveals the level of affection that must have existed between father and son. It states:

> Know ye, that I, Erastus Dudley of Guilford in the county of New Haven and the State of Connecticut for the consideration of love and good will and service rendered to my full satisfaction by Luther F. Dudley, my son, of said Guilford, do give, grant, bargain, sell, and confirm unto the said grantee a certain tract or parcel of land situated in said Guilford in the society of North Guilford, containing one acre, bounded north and east on my own land, south and west on the turnpike roads, together with the dwelling house, and other buildings there on standing...

The house that Luther was given has been remodeled and altered over the years but the original two story structure still mirrors the original Federal style home popular in Guilford during the first thirty years of the 19th century. It may have been the original home of Erastus but more research needs to be done to ascertain that. This larger structure certainly would have housed the large family of Ruth and Erastus more comfortably than the older home just to the north but this raises some questions. If this was the original home of Erastus and Ruth, then did they share the home with Luther and his new wife until the present Dudley Farm house was built in 1844? Since that house also was also shared from the outset with their son Nathan and his new wife it can be assumed that Erastus and Ruth might have been comfortable with that type of living arrangement. If this was the case, then who occupied the small home across the Durham Road from the mill site? Since Luther was the first of their children to marry other than his twin, none of the other five children would have been in a position to establish their own household. Did Erastus build the new home for his son as a wedding gift? He does this later in the case of the Dudley Farm house. As for Luther's house today, the casual observer will notice that the turnpike as it exists today (Route 80) is now to the north of the house as it was rerouted during the early 20th century.

The land transaction between Erastus and his son shows some insight into Erastus, his character, and his relationship with his son. His giving of a home to his son for "the consideration of love and good will and service" seems a far cry from the type of relationship his grandfather Jared and father Luther had. Was this a manifestation of cultural changes taking place within the time period or simply a window into who Erastus was? As we will soon see, Erastus would follow a different path than his grandfather when it came to his family and opportunities. Perseverance had its rewards.

By 1841, Erastus Dudley was 58 years old, head of a large family, and apparently quite prosperous by the standards of the day and the community. The tannery was well established and was generating enough income for four of his sons to be involved there as tanners. Yet mysteriously, his oldest son, thirty year old James Harvey Dudley, is not mentioned in any of the documents associated with the tannery or any later records that recorded land transactions among the family members. He also does not appear in any of the Guilford Land Records. James was the third child of Ruth and Erastus and was born in 1811. Genealogical searches done by a number of Dudley family researchers since the late 19th century have found little information about him other than his birth date, 11/4/1811 and his marriage to Eliza Bray, date unknown. Judging by the inclusive and supportive role Erastus apparently played within his family, the absence of his eldest son is surprising. Was there a falling out between them? Did James follow many of the family's relatives south or west as part of the great migration out of New England taking place at the time? Was he drawn to the sea and a different life as so many of the young men of the community had for generations?

It is clear that by 1841 Erastus was still operating his grist and bone mills and hoped to continue so "...during the full term of my natural life..."[6] These two operations were obviously his focus and represent his connection to the past and the future. The grist mill, the long established family business, seemed by 1841 more of a sentimental nod to the past than a money making operation. There is no doubt local farmers still brought their corn and grain to Erastus to grind into flour but the volume would have greatly declined and most processed would have been for local consumption there no longer being a market outside of the community.

Following the construction of the new dam, the location of the mill may have been moved onto the structure and utilized either the western or middle raceways built into it. Because so much of the site has been severely eroded, the exact placement there is purely conjecture. However, what is left does reveal some clues. The part of the dam that once spanned the middle and eastern raceways is now completely gone. This 24^{ft} wide breach in the dam has washed away much of the evidence with it over the years. But approximately 20^{ft} of the mill site remains between the breach and the spillway of the dam to the west. The building that was located here would have been rather substantial, since the dam width was originally 40^{ft} from north to south and 50^{ft} from the eastern end of the breach where the most easterly raceway would have been and the spillway to the west. Once again the size of the mill building is conjecture but if it encompassed the middle and west raceways it would have been at least 30^{ft} wide from east to west and at least 20^{ft} from north to south. Within it, the two raceways are separated by 12 ^{ft}. The most westerly is the best candidate for the gristmill location due to its remaining size. This 8 foot wide, 6 foot deep stone lined trench then drops down another 3^{ft} to a total depth of 9^{ft}.[7] This is the probable location of the water wheel described earlier in Chapter 6.

The bone mill during the 1830's and 40's would have been a rather lucrative enterprise for Erastus. Utilizing a number of water powered saws and lathes, he would have produced bone material to be shipped to the many small bone implement manufacturers located all across the region and especially along the lower Connecticut River valley. By collecting and purchasing the bones of local livestock when their owners brought in hides for the tannery, Dudley would cut them into small workable pieces called plugs and blanks that he must have then sold to regional manufacturers to be made into handles for cutlery, combs, buttons, piano keys and countless other items we now use plastic for. With bone the plastic of the 19th century, Erastus had a ready and growing market. Due to the fact that no bone buttons or handles have been found on the site, which is usually the case where they were manufactured, the Dudley's were apparently content with the role of supplier of the raw material. The power for his machines would have come from a water wheel located in the middle raceway. This race has been completely destroyed and now forms the western end of the 24 foot breach. The footing stones for the raceway still can be seen in the stream bed, carefully placed cut sandstone blocks on which the walls of the raceway would have been built.

Ruth knew he was planning something. She could see it in her husband's eyes lately when he spoke to one of the boys. She saw it in the way he looked about the tanyard and how he had reviewed their accounts, over and over at times humming that new tune he had heard the young Billy Norton play on his fiddle the last visit to court their oldest, Mary Louisa. Something was definitely in the air she thought and with the Christmas holiday approaching she could wait no longer.

"Erastus" she teased, "I know your moods. The time for your secrets has passed as this family's welfare is my concern as well. The Lord knows I do not harry you when it comes to your musings, but if there is a scheme to be hatched then the time has arrived for an opening." Erastus fussed with a log, pretending not to hear as they sat by the fire in their snug little home. But his smile betrayed him as he leaned towards her with a sparkle in his eye.

"So it is secrets I am keeping?" he asked through a feigned wince of pain.

"Old man" Ruth replied, "Thirty years hold no secrets." "Tis a very long

time I have watched your thoughts brew and when they boil from the pot they'll be cleaning to be done." As she scolded he watched her face seeing only the young girl he had married so long ago.

"You have probed the enigma and the truth should be told" he said wryly. "The scheme is a simple one for you and for me. For our sons have proved worthy of our trust and confidence."

Ruth glared in annoyance for his evasion was clear. "I am not a mouse to be toyed with dear cat" she sternly responded. "Your obstinate ways shall be the death of me yet".

Erastus took her left hand in his and held it to his heart saying "Tis perseverance you mistake for an obstinate streak. I have penned a document I would like you to read and with your blessing tomorrow, we shall share it with our sons."

What Ruth Dudley would have read that evening would have been later recorded in the Guilford Land Records[8]. In it, dated December 24, 1841, Erastus turned over the tannery to his four sons, Luther, Erastus, Ebenezer, and Nathan. It reads as follows:

I Erastus Dudley of the town of Guilford in the county of New Haven and the state of Connecticut, for the consideration of $2500 received to my full satisfaction of Luther F. Dudley, Erastus F. Dudley, Ebenezer F. Dudley, and Nathan C. Dudley all of said Guilford do give, grant, bargain, sell, and confirm unto the said granted their heirs and assigns forever my Tanyard, Tannery, Currying, and other tools, and Bark Mill in said Guilford with the land and the privileges there to belonging bounded North on the land of Timothy Fowler, East on the Guilford and Durham Turnpike, South on the Essex and Fair Haven Turnpike, and west on the land of Timothy Fowler and the land of Henry Fowler. Containing three acres or less with the rights and privileges of the pond connected there with reserving to myself the right to enter on the said premises and to use and improve the Grist Mill and the Bone Mill connected there with, during the full term of my natural life and other privileges necessary to the full enjoyment of said rights reserved, and also reserving to myself and my heirs forever the horse barn and hog pound on said premises and the land on which the same stand twenty feet round them not interfering with the tan vats.

Not only does this transaction describe what was actually on the property at the time, it also sheds light on Erastus and his thoughts. Carefully delineating what his sons would now own, Dudley had also made it clear to keep control of his grist and bone mills, the horse barn, and hog pound. His sons were to own the tannery, the dam, and mill pond. The sum of $2500 was substantial for the time and speaks rather explicitly of how lucrative the tannery was. His sons, who were identified as tanners by then, must have all been experienced at the trade and thus eager to take on their new roles as owners. Erastus, in developing the site beyond the grist mill he had inherited from his grandfather, had begun the tannery with the hope of firmly establishing his family's future. With its operating profitably, he apparently felt it time to return to what he identified with more; farming and the grist mill. His only continued embrace of the present was the bone mill which could continue to provide him with the capital needed to soon build his new home on the hill overlooking the mill pond and the wherewithal to enter the next phase of his life; as merchant and banker of North Guilford. Erastus was reaping the harvest of perseverance.

Interlude Number Seven

(The following essay appeared in the Dudley Farm Newsletter Farm News, *Fall 1999. In it I wrote about the drought of 1999 and how droughts in the past would have impacted the Dudley's and their mill operations).*

Surviving the Drought?

As we all know, the remnants of Hurricane Floyd in early September brought to an end the Great Drought of the Summer of 1999. The drought that began for all intents and purposes in the late spring, persisted throughout the summer wreaking havoc with gardens, farms, and wells throughout the region. The effects of the drought were the usual topic of conversation Saturday mornings at the Farmer's Market and often as an ice breaker when conversing with strangers one met along the way. Weather calamities or at least problems always tend to bring us together, to open us to others, and give us pause in our daily routines.

In our busy, high tech world there were certainly people who may not have noticed the lack of rain and went about their lives as usual. As long as those vegetables appear at the local super store and water flows from the faucet, who cares?

During the 19th century, a spell of dry weather like the spring and summer of 1999 would have meant disaster. In a society more heavily dependent on local food production, hunger for many would surely have followed later in the year. Farmers, always hard strapped to make ends meet, would have been pushed to the limit. Economic disaster and loss of the family farm might have been the result.

The farmers would not have been the only ones to suffer at the hands of the drought. The 19th century was dependent upon water to power their mills and factories and the equation was simple; no water = no power = no work. A summer like the one that just passed would have resulted in massive layoffs and shut downs of mills and factories. The Dudley family mills and tannery along the West River across the Durham Road from the farm would not have been immune. The shallow dam that stored water in the millpond for the gristmill, bone mill, and tannery to use would not have held up to such a prolonged dry spell. A walk to the mill site would have made the problem obvious—a dry river bed and a puddle of a millpond would have halted all activity. What problems would the Dudley family have faced and how would they have overcome them?

The Dudley family most certainly would have banded together and worked to overcome the challenge. They realized that they had to face the future together in order to survive. In many ways we are much more fortunate than those who faced droughts in the past. For most of us, the drought was an inconvenience or topic of conversation. The rains finally came and the drought ended. For the Dudley Farm, the metaphor of the drought is important. We, the members of the Farm, are like the rain; without us the Dudley Farm cannot grow and prosper. The Farm needs your commitment and energy to continue our mission of preserving the past for future generations. Let's keep the Dudley Farm growing and not let it end like so many drought stricken family farms in the past.

Chapter Eight
Building on Success

Don't aim for success if you want it;
just do what you love and believe in,
and it will come naturally.
— DAVID FROST

T he second half of the 1990's represented a high water mark of sorts for the evolving Dudley Farm. Like the Dudley family in the 1840's, the Foundation faced the future with optimism and pride born of accomplishment and success. By the end of 1996 the Dudley Farm appeared well on its way towards living up to the vision established in the mailing to "preserve, restore, and operate as a historical, educational, and recreational resource" for the community and beyond. Membership was growing as was interest. Donations of items the farm could use for display were coming in on a regular basis. The high school class successfully completed its second full year and programs and workshops were beginning to be offered on various aspects of farm and country life. But beneath these signs of success were nagging questions and persistent problems.

Like so many non-profit organizations, the Dudley Foundation was chronically short on cash. Although membership was now firmly established and a pattern of yearly renewal was begun that year that would ask members to renew every October, overseeing this process and creating a large enough member base to allow the farm to pay its bills was proving difficult. Finances dominated every meeting the board of directors held and sometimes these discussions became quite heated.

There was so much to do in terms of just restoring and repairing the house to reflect the year 1900 that the list of basic must do's became no more than a wish list. Moving forward was an agonizing exercise in determination enveloped by frustration. Yet we all kept plugging, relying on one-another for strength and support, each doing what we could to help; thinking creatively, doing the little things, and always looking for a way.

At this point, a private non-profit in Guilford stepped forward to help. A trust established by the descendants of another branch of the Dudley family from North Guilford donated to the farm a sum substantial enough to help set us on a more sound financial footing. Although no longer residents of Guilford, the trust members still retained property in North Guilford and saw the creation of the Dudley Farm as an extension of their family's historic commitment to the community and the Dudley family's overall legacy. This gift came just as work within the house needed to be completed and the restoration had moved to the finishing stages. Plaster walls had been patched, paint had been applied, and the ceilings patched and resurfaced. Together with a donation from the North Guilford Fire Company's Ladies Auxiliary, replacing the wall paper in the dining room, parlor, and what was to become the library could now take place.

The wall paper that had been in place when David Dudley had died covered every room in the house and had finally been removed. Pealing and faded would have been a generous description and the process of painstakingly removing it had revealed as many as four or five layers fused together. As each layer was stripped, an example of each was saved and catalogued and for the three main rooms of the house patterns that were close to what had been in the room around 1900 were researched and ordered. The second floor rooms were repainted white with the hope of someday being able to repaper them as well.

The grounds of the farm continued to be restored to reflect the end of the 19th century as work on the flower and herb gardens moved forward and the organic gardening project firmly took hold. Students and volunteers continued to clean up and in a few cases dismantle for safety reasons some of the smaller outbuildings with a plan to one day recreate them. A small tractor shed, which stood in the heart of the lawn area behind the great gray barn and on the crest of the hill overlooking a century old maple tree, was the first to undergo a facelift. It was determined by the board of directors that the shed could serve as an ideal classroom and meeting space for workshops and demonstrations that were now taking place at the farm and with the help of students from the Dudley Farm class and volunteers from the foundation was given new life. An important milestone of sorts, the restoration of this dilapidated structure into a multifunctional space became a visual reminder of progress.

It was in situations like these that the network within the Fire Company that thrived on self-reliance, was at its best. Led by Henry and Bob, members of the Fire Company could get just about any job done through contacts and acquaintances, often at little or no cost to the farm. Whether it was a load of stone, donated concrete, or plumbing to be fixed, they knew who to "stop by and see". They also devoted countless hours themselves doing the hard work necessary to keep the farm going and along with Doug, were tireless in their efforts. By the annual meeting of the Dudley Foundation that October, the future of the farm looked limitless.

1997 began with continued optimism and growth and proved to be an important transitional year as the Dudley Farm became an active and vibrant museum, educational resource, and community gathering place. In late 1996, the Guilford Foundation, another local non-profit whose mission was to assist in local community projects, had given the Dudley Foundation a grant to assist in its continued efforts to restore and operate the farm. The Guilford Foundation was created in 1975 to give citizens of the town a functional vehicle for easy and effective philanthropic giving. This gift also proved timely as by the annual meeting that October it had become more than clear that the farm would not be able to survive on membership alone and that a new financial scheme was needed. The Dudley family trust gift and the Guilford Foundation Grant fortunately bought some time for the board of directors to find a more permanent financial remedy—but what?

It was to be his crowning achievement and a lasting memorial to his prosperity and that of his family. Erastus and Ruth had begun planning its construction a number of years earlier but now with the pending marriage of their youngest son Nathan it seemed like the time was right.

"It will be a grand house and a wonderful gift for the newly betrothed",
Ruth said of the plan just prior to the start of building. With its seven rooms,
three up and four down, the home was a spacious mansion by the standards
of North Guilford and sat on the hill overlooking the mills, nestled half way
up the sloping ridge to the northeast. From there it dominated the whole of
what was now called Dudleyville. Regal in its dignity, it loomed over all
who passed on the Durham Road and proclaimed the prosperity of the its
owners.

It had taken eight months to complete but was ready for the wedding
day. Erastus had seen to every detail and had even joined in the work more
than he should have. At age 61, Ruth had worried about his crawling up
onto the timber frame to assist in the framing, or the roof to help shingle.
As was his custom, he had teased Ruth for her concern and proclaimed he
would rest their first night in the house. She had asked her sons to rein him
in if they could but their efforts were as fruitless as her own. Her suspicion
was they enjoyed the freedom of his absence from the tannery and were not
as forceful in their pleas for moderation as she had hoped. Only Nathan,
when told of their plan to have him and his bride, Sophronia, move to the
new home once wed, had harried him often but to no avail. To Erastus, it
was more than a house and he would not be kept from it.

The house Erastus built was completed in 1844 and it is assumed that
he and Ruth, along with Nathan, moved in prior to his marriage to
Sophronia Annis Rossiter (1822-1890) on December 9th. All nine of
their other children had already married and established their own
homes by then, the last being their youngest, twenty one year old Abi-
gail Ann that August. What thoughts must have raced through their
minds as Ruth and Erastus began this new phase of their lives in the
spacious new home on the hill, we can only imagine. After all those
years in a crowded, noisy house filled with the chatter and drama of
family life, their new home, strangely quiet and cavernous in size, must
have suited that transition in an odd yet exciting way.

It is easy to see the 1844 house of Erastus when one looks at the
Dudley Farm house today. Strip away the large addition to the left
(north) and the small addition and porch on the southern and eastern
sides, his stands as the present home's core. At first sight this is typical
of many built throughout the region during the 1840's by individuals

of affluence and means and even by today's standards is impressive in its size and design. It has however, many features that identify it with what was still a rather traditional and conservative culture in North Guilford and as one of the community's most prominent citizens, not surprisingly embraced by Erastus. After all, despite his success in other economic ventures, he still saw himself as a landed farmer and member of the traditional gentry first and foremost.

The first clue to this conservative strain is the basic floor plan and shape of the home. In essence, the plan is that of a traditional Colonial style house built in Guilford, for by then close to 200 years. The floor plan is arranged around a central chimney that allows for four rooms on the first floor and in this case, three on the second. By the 1780's in Guilford, newer homes had been replacing this design with two chimneys arrayed on either side of a central hallway that ran through the home from front to rear. This form first appeared in what is called the Georgian style and continued throughout subsequent styles as well. Thus by the start of the 19th century, a central chimney plan was popularly seen as outdated. The Georgian style itself had been eclipsed by the varied arrangement of rooms and design inherent to what were later named the Federal and Greek Revival styles. The homes of Erastus's sons, Luther and Erastus F. just to the south, are good examples of these. Yet by 1840, these were being replaced by the newly emerging Gothic and Italianate styles. Dudley would certainly have seen all of these and might easily have chosen one for his home's design, but as a testament to his success he chose to look to the past instead of the future.

The traditional floor plan of the house also contains an element that the 17th century ancestors of Erastus would have recognized and been comfortable with, an interior porch. During the 17th and 18th centuries, this small room, located to the front of the central chimney stack and between the two main front rooms was the arbiter between public and private space within the house as well as the exterior and interior. Traditionally, when a guest or visitor arrived, they would first enter the home into this space where the owner would decide whether they would be welcomed into the less formal and family oriented room to one side called the hall or a more formal room used for ceremonial and special occasions to the other side called the parlor. The parlor in a Colonial home, contained the family's most expensive and formal furniture and possessions. It was a room designed and decorated to impress and therefore only used when special guests arrived or occasions warranted.

The porch also contained the main staircase to the second floor and was usually highly detailed in its construction and design. The staircase dominated the space and was also a traditionally visual symbol of the family's wealth as it proclaimed not only the fact that the home contained a second floor, but that they had the means to afford the often ornate carpentry necessary to build it. This is the case in the Dudley house porch as even today the ornately turned and curved banister draws comments from visitors.

Although the two rooms to either side of the porch by the time the house was built would have no longer functioned in their traditional colonial manner, one still can get a sense of the past when looking at their design and detail. One served as a more formal space, today's library, and the other a less formal family space, today's Victorian parlor. Also, unlike their colonial antecedents, they are both bathed in natural light from the windows which gives them a warm, comfortable, and inviting feel.

To the rear of the house Erastus built, are what would have been the two most used and functional rooms for the family; the kitchen and dining room. The kitchen, located behind the present library extended across ⅔'s of the back of the house and was the domain of Ruth and soon Sophronia as well. It would also have been the most lived in space within the house for it was here where food preparation and cooking would have taken place along with many of the other tasks that took up most of a woman's day. Just as today, it was also the social center for family life. The kitchen has however, been reduced in size with the installation of a bathroom at some point during the 20th century as well as a closet on the northern end. Additional space was also separated to create a late 19th century pantry which probably did not exist when the house was first constructed. The pantry, closet, and bathroom may have once been part of another room, either a bedroom or a storage room called a buttery during colonial times. The buttery eventually evolved into the late 19th century pantry and was commonly found in colonial homes.

The dining room to the south of the kitchen and directly behind the present Victorian parlor was not only a vital and heavily used space within the home; it is also one of the most formal spaces, especially when compared with the casual and functional space of the kitchen. It was here that Ruth and Erastus would have hosted gatherings of family and friends and even today it exudes a warm and welcoming charm. This is the first room most visitors enter when touring the house and though the décor today is a bit sparse, they almost always mention the charming atmosphere; due no doubt to the lingering feelings of joy and past laughter that once resounded within it.

One special feature found in the room is the faux finish on the woodwork and trim that graces it throughout and gives it a simple yet sophisticated elegance. Probably the work of an itinerant painter, this type of finish gives the woodwork a marbleized look that was popular throughout the mid to late 19th century. It was common for painters to travel from town to town plying their trade and since this was a specialized skill, it was one a small community like Guilford would not have been able to support. It is unusual to find an example in a rural location such as the Dudley house since this fashionable finish was most often found in cities where there was enough wealth to support the trade. In many cases, surviving examples were long ago lost to changes in fashion and paint and the fact that such a fine example survived in the Dudley house is rare indeed. That either Erastus or later Nathan went to the trouble and expense to have the finish applied is a testimony to their pride in their home and what it meant to them.

The fact that the finish survived the restoration of the house by the Dudley Foundation is also a testimony to the ability of the board of directors to make sometimes difficult and contentious decisions. What to do about the woodwork in the dining room was a sensitive topic of debate as the restoration of the house continued during the late 1990's. The surviving finish was worn, scraped, and filthy and in many places missing. To make matters worse, the finish on the large pocket door that separated the dining room from the parlor needed to be restored as well which would add substantially to the cost. This eight foot wide door was a focal point for both rooms when closed and an important feature for the house in general when slid open or closed into the wall. Tempers flared as the board divided between those who opted to paint and those who wanted to spend the money necessary to maintain the historical integrity of the finish and thus the room and door. Early on the board had adopted a simple rule when it came to restoration: save what can be saved, replace what can't. The problem was, for every board member there was a different interpretation of the rule and this was never made clearer than with the battle over the finish.

Fortunately at the time there was a craftsman in Guilford who did restore vintage woodwork, Robert Coale of *Old World Finishes (now masterfinisher.com)*. Following a rather raucous series of board meetings, the vote to proceed with restoring the finish was approved and in the fall of 1999, Robert was able to spend the almost three weeks needed to complete the job. I described the restoration process in the March, 2000 *Farm News*:

> The preservation and restoration process was quite lengthy and required a number of steps starting with cleaning the woodwork of years of grime and soot. The next steps involved adding, matching, and blending color to damaged areas while allowing the 'age' of the original finish to still come through. This required a number of steps using 'old world' powders and techniques. The remaining steps included a continued blending, shellacking, and in some cases regraining to match the original finish.
>
> The goal of the project was not to re-do or replace the original finish, but to preserve and repair what was there in order to save the character of the room that has existed since the turn of the last century. The result is a feast for the eyes as the woodwork now glows with the beauty and patina of yesterday while being preserved for tomorrow.

This was the first legitimate attempt of the board to reach out way beyond its expertise and network to take on a serious attempt at historic preservation and restoration and was a watershed of sorts. There would never be the same degree of contention again when it came to saving the historic fabric of the house, barns, and land. The faux finish made it clear—saving the farm was more than just fixing her up and making her look good. The legitimacy of the farm as a museum and piece of history was at stake and it had to be done right. The finish is still one of the most remarkable features of the Dudley home.

Despite the traditional floor plan of the house, there was a radical and important difference in the home compared to its colonial ancestors; the central chimney. A traditional Colonial house was usually built around a large central chimney. This massive structure allowed for the placement of fireplaces in the three main rooms on the first floor, the hall, parlor, and kitchen. Often there were also fireplaces in the rooms on the second floor as well. The central flue for the smoke to exit could be as wide as two feet square and the chimney itself, in order to accommodate the large flue, was often four to five feet square as it made its way from the first floor through the second and roof. These massive chimneys still form a feature that distinguishes Colonials from later styles. To support the weight of the chimney and fireplaces, a large stone structure was constructed below the chimney in the cellar called a chimney stack. Often eight, ten or more feet square, the stack dominated the cellar space and was often the reason why a cellar was built to begin with. The house frame was consequently built around the stack and the chimney above and thus an important clue as to whether or not a home had an original central chimney with fireplaces.

The fireplaces within the central chimney provided the main source of heat and were used for cooking and baking in a colonial home. They were highly inefficient for both uses as the majority of the heat went up the stack with the smoke. Fireplace design changes during the 18th century tried to mitigate the problem but with limited success. By 1820 however, fireplaces were quickly being replaced by cast iron heating and cooking stoves. First developed in the 1740's, these more efficient sources of heat and for cooking were slow to gain acceptance, especially in rural areas. But by the early 19th century the expense of a dwindling wood supply coupled with a drop in the overall cost of a stove due to more efficient manufacturing resulted in their growing popularity and acceptance. The Dudley's appeared to embrace this new technology as an inspection of the framing around the central chimney shows a much smaller chimney and stack than that of a colonial style home with a large stack for fireplaces. Each stove was vented into the chimney with a metal pipe that carried the smoke into the central flue which was much smaller in size than its colonial counterpart.

The Dudley's had placed a wood stove for heat in each of the two front rooms on the first floor and apparently a larger cooking stove in the kitchen. That stove, used for both cooking on the top surface and baking within it, represented a significant improvement over the traditional fireplace and beehive bake oven. The stove also provided heat for the kitchen and the dining room. Later, when a room was added to the rear of the dining room and the room itself expanded in size, a second chimney was added to provide for the placement of a stove for additional heat. Exactly what type of stove the Dudley's first used in the kitchen is impossible to tell but a good sense of what it might have been like in the room at the time can be seen today with the early 20th century version of a cook stove that now graces it.

It became fashionable during the 1830's and 40's when cast iron stoves were first installed in existing homes to seal up the existing fireplace while leaving the surrounding mantel. In an interesting nod to fashion, Erastus had mantels with false fireplaces built in both front rooms and later when the stove was placed in the dining room one there as well. The illusion that a fireplace once existed is a striking and dominant feature in each room and further links him to his traditional roots. It turns out the Dudley's were fine with tradition unless the efficiency and convenience of cast iron stoves outweighed it.

Erastus had approached his son Erastus F. early on when he and Ruth had decided to build their new home to talk about the design of the house he had built a number of years previous on the west side of the Durham Road across from the home of Luther. Called Greek Revival, the design emulated an ancient Greek temple in style and shape, a popular symbol embraced by many Americans and symbolic of their view of themselves as heirs to the democratic traditions of the ancients. With its bold framed pediment and the gable side of the home turned to the road to become the front, the home did have the look of a temple as seen in the images he had viewed in books on the subject. His son had teased him of his interest, reminding his father of how he had questioned his decision as a bit more "ambitious and bespoken of airs" than was the norm.

"Father, why now the interest in such frivolous design?" he had jabbed in good hearted revenge.

"Was my gable but a spurious waste of a good man's wealth?"

"Indeed" was his reply.

"Yet I have come to understand the nature of the style and the meaning

it proclaims" said Erastus.

"Let us just say you have led me to enlightenment as a good son should".
With that they both laughed as they strolled up the path to the temple-like
doorway to the home.

"Father, I can retrieve the builder's plan books from the chest for your
use" Erastus F. suggested.

"Aye son, 'tis a good place to start".

As much as the interior of the house of Erastus spoke of the past, the
outside is another matter. In design the exterior boldly proclaims an
identification with the notion of America as the new Greece; the em-
bodiment of the ideals of democracy, individualism, and freedom. The
traditional center chimney shape is adorned with dramatic Greek Revival features resulting in a magnificent example of that style in form
and function. Yet for Erastus, it was more than that, it was also a statement about and verification of his role as family patriarch and his efforts to lead them into the future prosperous and secure. At a time
when so many local farms were failing and families were broken up to
be dispersed across the continent in a search for economic security, he
and his sons had defied the odds. This house would be his monument
to that and indeed it still is.

The front façade or face of the house is typical of its time with five
over five bays or openings; four windows and a center door on the first
floor and five windows aligned above those of the first on the second.
The windows on the second floor have classic early 19th century, double
hung sash with each sash made up of six panes. A nod to tradition, they
are the original windows in the house and their size and number bathe
the second floor in light. Those on the first floor may also be original
but are a style more typical of the post 1840 era, two double hung sash
made up of two large panes each. If they replaced earlier six over six
windows like those on the second floor, that replacement would have
taken place later in the 19th century when they became the norm.

Each window on the first floor has a window lintel or hood above
it, a typical Greek Revival feature and the area where the front wall
meets the roof, called the eave, has a wide Greek cornice or band running across. Each window also is graced with a full set of 19th century
green shutters that may in fact be original to the house and could be

closed when necessary. As a result, the façade of the house is simple yet elegant, stately, and dignified as it exudes the pride and confidence of its builders.

The most noticeable and prominent feature on the front of the house is the large Greek portico or exterior porch that dominates the façade. Held up by two large Doric columns, the roof of the portico extends outward and mimics the entablature or cornice of an ancient temple. The result is a striking image designed to suggest the power and majesty of the once ancient and now American ideals. The overall impression is one of timeless strength and confidence. On the gable or southern end of the house are other details inspired by Greek temples, a large triangular pediment that defines the roof line and mimics those found on ancient buildings and a rectangular window in the peak to allow light into the attic.

There are two later additions to the original 1844 house that will be addressed later, but taken as a whole the Dudley house is a great example of 19th century vernacular or local architecture. The fact that it survived into the late 20th century with few alterations is both a fortunate surprise and testimony to the traditional nature of the family. Luckily for us, the house in its relatively unaltered form helped make the idea of a museum possible and daily transports visitors back to another age.

Activity on the farm picked up dramatically during 1997 and in retrospect that year was pivotal to the farm's survival. I had taken on the role of president at the annual meeting the past October and soon was immersed in the daily details of the blossoming effort. The board had changed as well as new members were added and officers; vice president, secretary, and treasurer chosen in an effort to open decision making up to more foundation members. With renewed vigor we faced the upcoming year with eager anticipation.

That spring saw the first Saturday Farmers Market at the farm which has since become an institution in the area. A full calendar of well attended events, workshops, and demonstrations were held throughout the spring, summer, and fall, among them were herb workshops, grafting and twig furniture making. That February saw the farms first attempt at maple sugaring which would lead later in the year to the reconstruction of the Dudley's sugar house. By May, an acoustic music jam was being held the first Saturday of each month that eventually evolved into the farm's own Dudley Farm String Band. Work on the house had progressed to the point of being able to host tours and that fall we added volunteer docents on Saturdays. In the fall volunteers also began to staff the farm office, a room behind the dining room added some time in the 1860's, Monday through Friday a few hours each day. This group led by Evelynne Tichy and Loraine Ashman, began to sort through the complexities of managing the membership lists and giving tours to people who stopped by the farm. The yearly open house became the annual Farm Day that June at which the farm hosted events and exhibits that attracted over 800 visitors. As board members, we were all proud of what we had accomplished but still there was always the nagging problem of how to fund the farm so it could all continue.

Amidst this growth an opportunity for substantial long term development emerged that though full of promise and potential, exposed once again differences within the board as to the vision for the farm's future. Doug, always looking for opportunities to help the farm grow, had been in contact with Philip and Susan Catullo, owners of PMC Design Group who had recently bought the Munger Lumber Company property in the neighboring town of Madison. There the Munger family, related to David Dudley through his grandmother Martha, had owned and operated a number of businesses for over 200 years; from a farm to a boat building lumber yard to a commercial one. The family had decided to sell the property to the Catullo's who planned to build houses on the site and they wished to remove the several barns that stood on it. They had decided to donate the largest of the barns, a late 19th century, 30ft x 50ft structure, to the Dudley Farm.

This extraordinary gift would allow us to rebuild it on the farm's property, preferably on the site of the earliest barn that had been dismantled by the Dudley's in the 1960's. Initial thoughts were to use what instantly became known as the Munger barn as a display space, class room, workshop, and event and rental space for weddings, gatherings, and receptions. The idea was that the barn would provide a source of income for the foundation and thus alleviate the financial stress we were chronically operating under. Even though the barn was graciously being donated, the farm still needed to pay for its dismantling and storage until it could be rebuilt. Thus the problem; how were we to fund such a project when our shoe strings were already stretched to breaking?

Once again the board was thrown into turmoil as it quickly split into two opposing camps, one group, though recognizing the potential the Munger barn offered, saw no need for it at that time as it represented an expense the farm could just not afford. The other group saw the investment in the barn as an investment in the farm's future growth and just as adamantly argued for it. Emotions flared and the two sides hardened their positions as it seemed the chance to accept the gift from the Catullo's would disappear. Time was running out as PMC wished to move forward on developing the property and the other structures had already been removed. Just when it seemed the barn would fall to the developer's bulldozer, members George and Linda Curry stepped forward with a generous gift that partially funded the expense of dismantling it. This was enough to convince a slight majority on the board to use some of the precious few dollars the foundation had raised through membership to save the barn. Timber framer Gary Terwilliger and his crew were hired to carefully dismantle the barn, numbering each timber so that they could be reassembled at a later date. An old storage container truck was saved from going to scrap by the town and given to the farm to temporally store the frame and as the Munger barn arrived at the farm the rusting green trailer became the daily topic of conversation as visitors routinely asked "so what's in the trailer?"

While all the drama associated with the barn played out, another ambitious project began that fall as members of the Guilford Rotary volunteered their time and some funds to reconstruct the Dudley's sugar house which had collapsed around the stone "cooker". The debris had been cleared away the previous year and the cooker or oven had proven usable the past February when volunteers had done some sugaring on the farm. Organized and led by Doug, the Rotary members shaped the timbers and erected the frame on the footprint of the old house and soon an exact replica of what had once stood there, thanks to an old photograph, was ready for the upcoming maple sugaring season. Both these important projects, the saving of the Munger barn and the reconstruction of the sugar house, made it obvious that growth had its price. While furthering the farm's development, they had also exposed a rift in the foundation's leadership that would continue to play out in a continuing dispute over the very nature of the farm and how it might survive financially.

Interlude Number Eight

(The following essay appeared in the Dudley Farm Newsletter Farm News, *March 2000. In it I wrote about the tradition of maple sugaring in the region and on the Dudley Farm).*

February and March are traditionally maple sugaring time in Connecticut. Once considered a necessity, maple sugar was produced by local farmers throughout the 17th, 18th, and 19th centuries in place of the much too expensive cane sugar that was imported from the Caribbean. Maple sugar was used for sweetening, cooking, and eaten as a treat. It served as an important trade commodity for farmers and was vital to the survival of many families.

During the later part of the 19th century, maple sugar was no longer in demand as processed cane sugar became affordable and the sweetener of choice for most residents of Connecticut. For many farmers, maple sugar production simply stopped. For others, such as the Dudley's at the Dudley Farm, production switched to maple syrup, a "specialty" product that gradually grew in popularity. Like many other farmers during the late 19th and early 20th centuries, the Dudley's continued the traditions passed down since colonial times and produced, weather permitting, through hard work a bountiful crop year after year.

At the Dudley Farm we still demonstrate to members and the public as well as to visiting school children how maple sugaring took place 100 years ago. Trees are tapped, sap is collected, and it is boiled down using traditional methods in the sugar house. The present sugar house on the Farm is on the same spot the original one once stood. It was rebuilt a number of years ago by members of the Guilford Rotary Club.

Maple syrup production is still a major agricultural activity in Connecticut. Every year tens of thousands of gallons are produced for sale and our enjoyment. Although the technology employed may be more efficient and sophisticated, it still takes hard work and 40 gallons of sap to make a gallon of syrup. It is a labor intensive business that at times is more a labor of love than practicality.

At the Dudley Farm we still make syrup the way it was done 100 years ago. If we make enough to sell, we place it in 8 ounce bottles with a label that is a replica of the one used earlier in this century by *Nathan C.*

Dudley and Sons. The collecting, boiling, the sugar house, and the label all connect the present Dudley Farm to the past. When Nathan Dudley placed the label on his bottles of syrup, he was undoubtedly proud of what he had accomplished and hoped his sons would continue the traditions embodied in maple sugaring. In that regard, we the members of the Dudley Foundation are his heirs. It is now our responsibility to keep those traditions alive for the present and future. Your continued support is the sap that keeps the sweet syrup of tradition possible for future generations. Together, let's keep those sugar pans boiling!

Chapter Nine

Illusion of Success

The past gives you an identity and the future holds the promise of salvation, of fulfillment in whatever form. Both are illusions.
— ECKHART TOLLE

s 1998 began it became clear that the Dudley Farm was wrapped within the illusion of the past while struggling to find that of the future. Five years of hard work and steady progress had created a history of accomplishment and an identity that was transforming the farm into the Dudley Foundation's vision of "preserving, restoring, and operating the farm as a historical, educational, and recreational resource". Yet differences on the board of directors over the shape and extent of that vision had shrouded the illusion that a unified interpretation of that mission existed. Growth had begun to call into question the very nature of that future, a vision we all clung to somehow despite the differences. In the end, the promise of salvation would take many forms.

The successful growth of the farm as a museum, educational center, and community resource had made the operational model put in place by the Fire Company back in 1993 to run the farm no longer viable. Though none of us on the board may have wanted to address that issue, it was obvious to all. To compound the problem, we all had different perspectives on the cause and any possible solutions. The board of directors originally created to be an oversight committee had evolved by

1995 into a group that met weekly, sometimes for three or more hours managing the minutia associated with its day to day operations. It had also become a work committee that tackled each and every task, problem, and project that needed to be addressed and had proven with few exceptions, unable to consistently reach out to the greater membership of the foundation for help. Beginning in 1996, a series of proposals to develop volunteer committees to take on various aspects of developing, managing and working on the farm consistently collapsed leaving some board members and dedicated foundation volunteers to continue to carry the full burden.

The reasons for failure in this area were varied and numerous and as president at the time I found them frustrating and disheartening. Often it was due to a lack of coordination and organization by those involved, sometimes it was the unfortunate reality created by our modern society in which time is a premium that few can spare despite the best of intentions. Other times it was a manifestation of the culture of self-reliance brought to the farm by the Fire Company that discouraged outsiders and sought to minimize expenditures. Failure in this regard was also often the result of a growing mistrust within the board over the direction of growth though this was never articulated or discussed when brought up, but masked in a stony silence and reluctance.

As the year progressed it became increasingly apparent to some of us on the board that an operational change needed to take place and haltingly and at times emotionally, we discussed what form that change might be. Predictably, the board quickly split into factions, again centered on the shape and extent of that change. It was agreed, however that following a more museum focused model might be the best solution and by the fall a decision was made.

Another change had come to the farm rather dramatically the spring of 1997 with the decision by the administration at Guilford High School and the Board of Education not to continue the Dudley Farm Class. Despite its success, the reality of school budgets based on local tax dollars had made continuing the program in the view of the Superintendent of Schools and the High School Principal too expensive. Despite the fact that Tom and I had over 40 applicants for the 24 positions for the fall semester; a decision was made that with the town's new education budget as it was, it would be better if we both took on two classes back at the high school and thus each teaching more total students. We were as devastated as the students.

At the farm, the news of the demise of the high school class was met with surprise and disappointment just as plans were being formulated for the summer and fall. Gloom descended over most conversations only adding to the sense that suddenly we were taking steps backward and that a change of direction was now inevitable. In particular, the cancellation of the class seemed like a serious blow to the forward momentum of the farm as the students always brought with them an enthusiasm and energy that often lifted those around them who were working hard to restore and develop the farm. Suddenly one of the most important forces propelling that development was gone as were their eagerly helping hands. Tom and I were determined to not let it end.

Sophronia could not have been happier. The arrangement to move to the home of her in-laws had at first been met with some trepidation mixed with fear and anxiety. Now one year later, all had fallen into a comfortable compatibility. Ruth had welcomed her as a daughter and together they had become adept at handling the daily chores associated with running the household. Meals were cooperative but at times each family would tend to their own with a schedule often put forward by Ruth. Sophronia had teased her on the fact that such a device had been needed with her large family in a small home over the years and she had agreed it was a way of keeping her sanity. The spacious kitchen had afforded a degree of room that made most tasks workable and in time they had developed an instinctual working relationship.

For his part, Nathan had taken on the role of managing the family land holdings and happily commented he was always more suited to the life of a farmer than a tanner. He loved the sun on his face on a late June afternoon or the sweet smells of fresh mown hay when the ricks were just built. All in all, the mud on his boots and the sweat on his brow were like a balm to his soul and happiness and he thanked the lord each day for his good fortune.

Now with Sophronia expecting their first child, Nathan felt his purpose in life was becoming clear and that the future seemed as bright as the sunlight that caused him to squint as he gazed back towards the stately white house on the brow of the hill. "A wife and child" he mused to himself. "The Lord's plan is simple and beautiful to contemplate". Nathan thought of Sophronia, her face softly pinched in kindly expectation as she told him of the child.

"A child we shall have, Nathan" she had quietly told him that morning when he had come in for his breakfast after the morning milking was done. He remembered how his words had escaped him as he struggled to respond, muted by an overwhelming surprise fed by joy. "Husband", she prodded, "your voice will be needed to raise up a child, so mute will not do." As she took up his hands in hers, they laughed together.

Their commotion brought Ruth to the room from the parlor where she and Erastus had breakfasted earlier, both enjoying the breeze through the windows that warm late spring morning. A look at both faces had confirmed her suspicion as Ruth's hands joined with theirs in an embrace of pure happiness. "I knew dear daughter for the signs spoke of a child. This house will now truly be a home as the only thing lacking has been the sounds of the young."

Nathan knew of his mother's desire for a child in the home and how she relished her role as grandmother to his nieces and nephews. With that she embraced them both and implored them to tell Erastus the news. "Why mother, disturb him at the bone mill? You know when the wheel is turning he brokers no interruptions", Nathan said with a mocked look of concern.

"For news such as this, the wheel will stop" was her earnest reply.

Nathan and Sophronia would go on to have five children, four girls and one son. Their first, Annis Sophronia (1846-1919), was born March, 8, 1846 followed by Erastus (1849-1919), Lucy Elizabeth (1852-?), Catherine Brooks (1854-1885), and Mary Rossiter (1859-1883). For the next 70 years, from the arrival of Annis through the early decades of the 20th century, the Dudley home would not only be filled with the sounds of children's laughter, but three and sometimes four generations. It became a bustling and crowded place full of all the joy, drama, and trauma associated with family life.

The farm would eventually pass to their son Erastus, named I'd like to imagine, to the delight of his grandfather. Annis Sophronia would remain in North Guilford her entire life, having married Edwin Bartlett. Of the third child of Nathan and Sophronia, Lucy Elizabeth, little is known. Whether she married and left the area or spent her entire life in Guilford is uncertain, there is no record of her in the North Guilford

Cemetery where all the family members in the area are buried. To date genealogical searches have turned up no information. Catherine Brooks married Henry Lee Staples of Richmond, Virginia and died at the age of 30 in 1885. Also tragically, the youngest daughter of Nathan and Sophronia, Mary Rossiter, died in 1883 at the age of 24. By the time of Ruth's death in 1868, the household would have consisted of Erastus, who would outlive her another four years, Nathan, Sophronia, and all their children except for Annis who had married a month and a half earlier.

A wonderful photo of the Dudley family taken at some point in the 1860's, somehow survived in the house and was found among a number of discarded papers in an upstairs room shortly after the Fire Company took possession. It appears to be a family gathering; perhaps to celebrate a special occasion as all in the photograph are dressed in formal attire typical of the time. The setting is outdoors, in front of a white picket fence with a large bush or tree behind to the right in full summer foliage. Most are standing before the fence while eight are sitting in front of those standing. None of the twenty eight individuals are identified so exact identification of any of them is impossible, but it is fun to speculate who some may be.

Of those in the photograph, twelve are males and most appear to be in their 50's or older and one in particular I'd like to assume is Erastus. By the mid 1860's he was well into his 80's and the gentleman, sitting in front to the right of center, between two younger women, may be Erastus. Elderly, with thinning hair and a long beard, he seems an important person as others are obviously fussing and attending to him. Together they form a happy and caring image and you can almost feel the mood and hear the laughter associated with the occasion.

Many of the males in the group fit the age of the five sons of Ruth and Erastus as most would have been in their 50's and 60's by the mid 1860's. Of all ten men, one in particular fits the profile of Nathan, then in his mid-40's. He stands proudly to the center left of the group, the tallest one, his posture straight and confident, standing a bit forward and dominating the photograph. Trim and well groomed, he is mustached with close cropped hair as he intently faces the camera. Beside him to his left stands a stately woman, I'd like to think its Sophronia, elegantly dressed with her hair parted in the center and pulled back in the fashion of the time. A young man, about 16, sits in front of them and is probably their son young Erastus. One woman in particular catches one's eye. She is located standing towards the left side of the photo, turned slightly and smiling. She is older, full faced with a pleasant and kindly smile, gray hair pulled back in a tight bun. Elegantly adorned in a dark dress, she seems to be relishing the moment. Could this be Ruth?

The overall image presented by the photograph is a family secure in its position, confident in its future, prosperous, and happy. It is a moment in time that captures the supreme sense of success and the comfortable compatibility they obviously felt. A window through time, the image brings into focus the Dudley's at that exact moment when the future as envisioned by Erastus had become a reality.

At some point during the 1850's and possibly as late as the 1860's, the first addition to the house was built. The dining room was expanded to the south about six feet, an outside porch with spindled Gothic columns and railing constructed, and a new entry door leading from the new porch into the expanded dining room added. Behind the dining room and to the east, a room was added that, in later years, became the farm office. Whether or not that was its initial use is unknown and it may simply have served as a bedroom for the expanding household. The new entry door had two Gothic windows, rounded on the top to mimic Gothic arches found in medieval and particularly English buildings. This style had become increasingly popular in the United States starting in the 1840's and was a direct throw back to and identification with their British roots by the descendants of America's 17th century settlers. Increasingly alienated by the arrival on these shores of non-English immigrants, most notably Irish and German, the style gained in popularity as immigration increased. For the Dudley's, certainly not threatened by immigrants coming to Guilford, the use of the style was more likely just an attempt to be fashionable.

The bedroom on the second floor above the dining room was also expanded, and a fourth bedroom added above the new room below. On the second floor above the new first floor entry a Gothic window with a lovely curved arch was placed, bathing the room in westerly sunlight. The expanded room upstairs must have been welcomed by Nathan's growing family and was a significant sign of the cultural changes sweeping Connecticut that stressed a growing sense of the need for more personal space. The modern concept of the importance of the individual had arrived at the Dudley household.

The census of 1850 still lists the three Dudley sons, Luther, Erastus F. and Ebenezer as tanners. At some point after that date however, the tannery ceased to operate though Luther and Erastus F. were still listed as owners in 1860. There is no recorded account as to why, but economic conditions had certainly changed throughout the region by then probably forcing this radical decision. Increased competition from larger, more efficient tannery operations elsewhere in the state, region, and nation probably forced the closure as the American economy became increasingly industrialized and with that the scale of profitability shifted to larger and thus more profitable operations including those overseas. The Dudley tannery may have reached the limit of its ability to grow and thus they would have found it increasingly difficult to compete. According to an account found in the diary of Dudley descendant Sophia Rossiter Dudley published in 1940, the disappearance of the tannery coincided with the collapse of the regional shoe and leather industry at that time.[1] A story passed down through the descendants of Nathan and Sophronia's daughter, Annis Sophronia Bartlett, states that the tannery fell victim to disagreements between the three brothers resulting in the closure. Whatever the reason, the demise of the tannery must have come as a hard blow to the family resulting in a serious economic realignment.

The closure raises an interesting point. Up until that time, the Dudley family, dating back to the time of Captain William, had always functioned as a collective enterprise. The benefits were obvious; working together as a family unit allowed them all to succeed and put them in the best possible position economically. Erastus had followed this model beginning in the 1820's by developing what assets the family had with each male family member playing a specific role. This collective approach also gave them a level of security that protected them all during times of economic distress. Tasks could also be accomplished that were beyond the capacity of one individual, whether it was raising a barn, harvesting hay, or producing leather. By 1850, this was beginning to change.

In 1850, Erastus, as noted earlier, was listed as a merchant. This designation reveals that his economic position had evolved from that of being a producer; a farmer, miller, or tanner, to one who had amassed enough capital to buy and sell goods. As a merchant located at the cross road of two important highways, Erastus now supplied the entire area with the goods they might need while taking in kind items he could market there and elsewhere. His ledger, which can be seen in the Guilford Keeping Society's collection in the Guilford Free Library[2], reveals the extent of his dealings. The exact location of his "store" is uncertain but a small foundation almost directly across the Durham Road from the house may in fact be it. As he took on the role of merchant and banker, occasionally lending to local individuals, Erastus also led an economic transition within the family during which each male member began moving towards pursuing their own interests. Economically and collectively, the Dudley family by 1860 was becoming different than it had ten years earlier.

The 1860 census seems to document that transformation. In it all male members of the family are listed as farmers, including Erastus, so the tannery and the other mill operations were either closed or no longer an economic factor important enough to warrant a full time occupation. Exactly how long the grist mill and bone mill remained is unknown but their disappearance also likely occurred prior to that date. Despite these changes, all male family members list an increase in the value of their personal and real property, a curious development in light of the closings. Beginning in 1860 however, there is an increase in the number of land transactions between family members and others indicating a return to a more traditional measure of wealth; land.

How long the buildings that made up the tannery stood on the property after the closure is difficult to know but a survey of the area today seems to support the idea that they were probably dismantled and the material recycled which was a common practice of the time. Among the remnant stone foundations and the dam, no remaining wooden pieces associated with the structures have to date been found and also no visible sign of fire, to which many old and abandoned buildings succumbed to during the 19th and 20th centuries, has been noted. Interestingly as well, no photograph has ever surfaced of the mill site or the buildings from the 19th century which strongly suggests that they were removed some time prior to 1860 since by then photography was widely in use. An important clue to the time frame associated with the disappearance of the mill buildings and tannery is the 1864 land transaction between Erastus and his son Nathan recorded in the town land records. In it the only building mentioned standing on the lot is the horse barn previously referred to in the 1841 land transaction.[3] All the other buildings must have been removed from the site sometime between 1850 and 1864.

A close inspection of the main barn on the farm may help solve the mystery. Built in a number of sections, the earliest hay barn and stall section was probably built shortly after the construction of the house and is today behind and to the left of the larger front section. It is a traditional Connecticut or Yankee barn with the main door on the non-gable side, built into a hill to create space below for livestock stalls. Built in a traditional timber frame form, it is typical of most barns built during the later part of the 18th century and the first half of the 19th.

The front section of the barn however, is another matter. Larger than the rear portion, it is also a center bay Yankee barn but a look at the timbers show that much of the frame is from a recycled structure. Many of the timbers have non utilized pockets or mortises that once would have been fit to timbers positioned differently than their current use which is typical of timbers taken from other buildings. There are also some structural anomalies that are not common in the construction of barns at the time that were apparently the result of using parts of a frame originally used for another building. A good example is the curious support structure that is part of the cow milking area to the right of the center bay. If this portion of the barn was built in the 1850's or 1860's, it would have made perfect sense for the Dudley's to use portions of the tannery and mill buildings not only for expediency, labor, and cost reasons, but because timbers large enough for the construction of a barn of that size would have been in short supply owing to the level of deforestation that had taken place by then.

In the *Farm News*, Summer 2002, I wrote about the importance and use of the American barn, reprinted here to highlight the evolution of the Dudley barn and its importance to their livelihood as farmers.

Think of an American farm—past or present. What is the first image that comes to mind? Is it the bucolic pastoral scene complete with cows in a meadow? Is it tidy rows of crops waiting for the harvest? Is it a pleasing vista of fields framed by fences and stone walls? These images are certainly etched into many of our minds. But, if you revisit the scene, quickly this time, what do you see in the background, or maybe the foreground of your thoughts? A barn. Why? It is really quite simple; there is no image that symbolizes the very essence of what a farm is. When people think of farms, they see barns.

Barns today give a tangible link to our shared past, one perceived to be more simple and satisfying in its hard work wrapped around the rhythm of the seasons. As our society continues to move away from our agricultural roots at a frantic pace, the image of that past often becomes rooted in myth. As those myths become misty, the one tangible symbol of that past that we can see and touch are barns. We look at their majestic simplicity, the massive timbers of the frame, the faded paint on their siding, the romance, security, and strength they represent. But for those who depended on them for their survival, the barn was the center of their life, their security against an uncertain world.

Like all man-made structures, barns have evolved and changed over time. The first structures built by the early settlers of Guilford and surrounding communities were small utilitarian structures modeled after those built in England since the time of the Middle Ages. Built to house the livestock and grain of the farmer, these 17th and 18th century barns were fashioned out of timbers using traditional European framing techniques. Due to the abundance of timber in the region, barns quickly became taller than their English predecessors, often accommodating a second floor or "mow" for the storage of hay. The roof became less pitched to allow for this growth and the timber frame grew taller. The result was the development of the classic frame structure or "bents" that formed the sections of the timber frame as we know it today.

By the late 18th and early 19th centuries, barns in the region had evolved into the familiar form and usage recognized as the classic barn. In Connecticut, barns developed a distinctive shape and timber framed structure typified by the main barn still at the Dudley Farm. This form, called a "Connecticut" or "Yankee" barn, had a large central open bay accessed through large doors on one or both sides. This allowed for the easy unloading of hay wagons brought into the center bay. By storing hay in the second floor mows, the entire first floor was available for other uses. The central bay thus gave these barns and their frames a distinctive and functional appearance.

Barns continued to evolve as the needs of farmers changed during the 19th century. By 1900, barns had become larger and even taller with many auxiliary buildings or sheds attached to them. These multipurpose structures had areas for storing hay, a granary, horse stalls, a loafing area, milking area, and a workshop for making repairs on the harnesses and equipment needed to keep the farm running. This later era of the Connecticut barn can be seen in the main barn at the Dudley Farm. Frozen in time at the end of the 19th century, it displays the various stages of its growth and use.

What is now the central rear portion of the barn (behind the larger front section) was the original barn built in the 1840's when the current Dudley Farm house was built by Erastus Dudley. It was a "bank" barn that provided for animal stalls underneath and access to the main floor for storage of hay. The majestic front section of the barn was added some time during the 1850's or 1860's. It is built partly of recycled timbers that may have come from the grist mill and tannery buildings across the Durham Road from the farm. The rear portion of the barn that forms the "U" shape of the barnyard was used for grain storage and provided additional stalls for livestock. This part was added some time during the later part of the 19th century. In its entirety, the Dudley Farm barn is a unique survivor of the long tradition of barn evolution.

It was also during the 1850's that Erastus' original house on the property, was recycled as well. The house, discussed in Chapter 5, appears on a series of maps in the Guilford Free Library as the home of Ebenezer F. Dudley. Located on today's Dudley Farm on the 1852 and 1856 maps, by 1864 it had been moved north up the Durham Road to its present location just south of the intersection of County Road.

The moving of the house had become a major community event. Just about every team of oxen in North Guilford had been assembled and were standing in their usual fashion, calmly disinterested, awaiting direction. Their drivers on the other hand, were a different matter. They busied themselves expectantly while chatting with the spectators; neighbors, friends, and family, who had begun gathering just after sunrise for what promised to be greatest attraction of the winter. Ebenezer fretted and moved quickly about as the teams were positioned and the chains and hooks checked and rechecked. Would the frame that would serve as a carriage to act as a sled under the house hold up? Would the log rollers stand the strain and the whole negotiate the terrain? Would the frozen ground hold up to the weight?. What had always seemed a small house now loomed above him, gigantic in its size and scale.

All stood ready. As Ebenezer nodded to young Edwin Bartlett, who had volunteered to direct the move, the driver's cry rang out. "Giddup!" Edwin shouted, "giddup!"

With that the teams pulled and strained on their traces, chains snapping tight, as they slowly lurched forward, the house shuttering on its carriage. The crowd caught its breath as the house edged forward, slowly; first just a foot, then a yard, then a rod. A collective sigh followed by a cheer came from the gathering as the boys swarmed behind the creaking structure inspecting its footprint as men gathered the first of the log rollers to carry them forward.

"Tis a stout home son" said Erastus as he watched his old home move towards the hill. "In a fortnight she'll land at her new berth reborn".

"If the weather holds steady" replied Ebenezer as he winced at the sound of the groaning timbers. "Anxious I will be for fear of a thaw and the loss of solid ground".

Erastus scanned the cold, cloudless sky and agreed. "It is in the Lords hands."

Like most people in North Guilford at the time, the Dudley's believed that in the end, it was their God who determined their fate. They were willing to undertake extraordinary efforts in daily pursuit of a better life with a trust that their path was right and through hard work it was possible to succeed. Often events took a course beyond their control and it was then that they would stoically pick up the pieces and begin again, for they had no second option. For Tom and I that spring, it was the same. We had worked hard to help make the Dudley Foundation's dream of establishing an education center focused on the study of 19th century life a reality through the Dudley Farm class, only to have the fiscal realities of small town politics doom our best intentions. I can't help but think however that the tenacious quality that sustained the Dudley's motivated the two of us to somehow find a way to continue the program.

The illusion that a successful, innovative education program utilizing and helping a vital community resource was in and of itself enough to transcend the pitfalls so often associated with small town education politics had been burst. In a meeting with the superintendent to explore any possible way we might save the class, it was reiterated that all local options were gone. Perhaps, he suggested, we might apply for a grant from the Connecticut Department of Education. With this the only possibility, Tom and I quickly dove into the complex world of grant writing.

With exactly three weeks to apply to the Department of Education, we decided to focus on what we thought would be our strongest option, an Interdistrict Cooperative Grant that would allow neighboring school districts to send students to the farm in a broader attempt to expand the reach of our goal to teach students about 19th century life. The grant would cover $2/5$ th's of Tom and my salaries and some supplies, freeing the school district of any cost. The Dudley Foundation would host the students and receive the benefits of their presence and efforts. We were told not to get our hopes up.

The goals as written in the grant were the following:
+ To increase student appreciation of the past in a hands—on environment.
+ To provide an opportunity for all students to learn in a setting that encourages cooperation and collaboration.
+ To increase technology skills through interdisciplinary activities.
+ To improve student understanding of diversity through shared interdistrict experiences.

Called the *Back to the Future Program*, we hoped to encourage urban, suburban, and rural school districts to experience the Dudley Farm together in order to build through collaborative activities, a deeper understanding of diversity. The appeal would be to all grade levels, kindergarten through high school, with an emphasis on younger students for logistical reasons. A group of between five and ten Guilford High School students would also come to the farm each day as part of an independent study program and assist Tom and me with school visits. With the blessing of the superintendent and the Dudley Foundation, we hand delivered our application to the state office.

Within a short time Tom and I were informed by the Superintendent's Office that our application for a grant had been approved. Our education program would be saved even if the emphasis had now changed from working exclusively with high school students on the study and restoration of the farm to using it purely as an educational resource for local and regional students. We were elated. A brochure describing the program for students was quickly put together by us and sent to schools in town as well as across the region. Schools in the surrounding communities of Clinton, Madison, Regional School District 18, Groton, and New Haven signed on to the program along with Guilford schools and by the end of the fall semester of the 1997-8 school year Tom and I, along with our Independent Study students, had hosted over 2000 students. The dream of turning the Dudley Farm into a true regional educational resource was coming true.

With the program in full swing that autumn, a new feeling of energy and sense of direction returned to the Dudley Farm. The board of directors, still grappling with financial and organizational issues, welcomed new members Janet Dudley and Dave Generoso as well as a full slate of elected officers; myself as president, Joan Stettbacher as vice president, Linda Curry as treasurer, and Jerri Guadagno as secretary. Doug Williamson, Don Homer, Buster Scranton, Bob Ashman, Henry Tichy, and Tom Leddy remained on the board. With new vigor, we moved forward on the two most pressing problems; the financial viability of the foundation and a new administrative plan. Both it turned out were intertwined.

During the summer, Doug had been working behind the scenes to bring about an intricate property acquisition and swap that would bring the farm in the end a degree of financial stability that up to this point was elusive. Charlie Barrows, a good friend of David Dudley had recently died and given 15 of his 40 acre farm on neighboring Hoop Pole Road to his niece, Alison Haber. The rear 25 acres he willed to the Dudley Foundation. Knowing that her uncle and David had been close friends, Alison approached Doug with the idea of either selling or somehow granting the rest of Mr. Barrow's farm, which included a house and barns, to the Dudley Foundation. The idea was immediately embraced by Doug who saw it as an opportunity for the Foundation to acquire another farm with the idea of renting it to a tenant and thus securing an income other than that from donations and membership. It would also save the Barrow's Farm from development and connect it with open space already under the stewardship of the Guilford Land Conservation Trust. But it would all be tricky for the Dudley Foundation did not have the resources necessary to bring this about.

Working with the Guilford Land Conservation Trust, a scheme was launched to purchase the property from Ms. Haber and save the land. From the start the idea was a controversial one for the board as many though sympathetic to the idea of acquiring and saving the Barrow's farm, felt that it would put the Dudley Farm in financial jeopardy as a mortgage would have to be secured for the property. The purchase of additional land was also seen as being outside the original mandate for the Foundation as agreed to by the North Guilford Volunteer Fire Company and that any decision to expand it should be subject to the Company's approval. Once again, the board was divided, each side believing that they represented the best interest of the farm.

As president, I found myself caught in the middle and pushed to move forward quickly in exploring the acquisition in a way that would be most agreeable to all board members. The goal was to preserve the land while securing some if not all for the Foundation to utilize as an income producing property. That meant the Dudley Foundation would somehow come into possession of the Barrow's house and other buildings there. The Guilford Land Conservation Trust, created in 1970 to acquire and conserve natural places for future generations in Guilford, had grown to become the largest town land trust in Connecticut owning and protecting about 2,500 acres. Supported by donations and membership, this proactive non-profit leapt at the opportunity to preserve more open space in town. If it all came together, the Barrow's Farm would be linked to the Dudley Farm by land already under the Trust's stewardship creating a parcel of more than 100 conserved acres between them.

The following proposal was put forward:

The Guilford Land Conservation Trust would purchase the 25 acre parcel from the Dudley Foundation. This would link it directly with their land to the west. The Dudley Foundation then would use the proceeds from the sale to go towards the purchase of the 15 acres that contained the house and barns that fronted on Hoop Pole Road owned by Ms. Haber. To assist in this process, two acres would be split off from the 15 and sold to provide additional funds for the purchase. The Dudley Foundation would then secure from the Guilford Savings Bank a small mortgage to complete the transaction.

The Dudley Farm would gain a rental property that would generate monthly income while preserving 13 acres of fields and woodlands for future use by the Foundation. The barns on the property could provide future storage for the growing collection of artifacts, livestock, and be used for activities. The entire 40 acre parcel would be connected to the Dudley Farm by a system of old roads and trails that ran through a preserve that included old growth trees and woodland, small ponds, streams, and several high lookouts on rocky outcrops. But for the Foundation, there were a few catches.

The Foundation would be taking a gamble by obtaining a mortgage, no matter how small, on the property. If the mortgage could not be paid, then would that put the Dudley Farm in jeopardy? Would the Fire Company ultimately be responsible? What would happen if there was a prolonged period without a tenant, could the Foundation afford the expense? What if major repairs needed to be done on the house and barns? Wouldn't this take away from the ability of the Foundation to continue work preserving the Dudley Farm? How would this purchase impact the long term financial well-being of the Foundation and impact future plans for the Munger Barn?

Discussions were lively to say the least as we explored the ramifications of the purchase. Was this in the end in the best interest of the Dudley Farm and its mission? A majority of the board thought it was and the decision was made to proceed. With tenants already secured, we moved forward and in the process helped preserve another piece of the past while creating a steady source of income for the Dudley Foundation that would put us on a more solid financial footing. But there were ramifications.

For a number of board members, the Barrows farm purchase represented a significant turning point. In retrospect it seems they felt that the Dudley Farm, as first envisioned in those early meetings back at the fire house, was moving in directions that they found uncomfortable and controversial and a degree of acrimony became evident. The lingering fact that the farm had outgrown the administrative model still being used, a farm director overseen by the board of directors, combined with the purchase, led to a number of confrontational meetings. Many on the board were frustrated, Doug as volunteer farm director was overwhelmed by the growing magnitude of the job, and overall the casual culture first brought to the preservation and running of the farm was now encumbering its operation. It was not a surprise when Doug announced his resignation.

Doug Williamson in many ways had been the heart and soul of the early effort to preserve the Dudley Farm and the fact that he would remain actively involved as a board member was a relief to many of us. His decision to step down it turned out, would free him to become more productive in his pursuit to contribute to the growth and development of the farm. But what form the future would take for the Dudley Farm was uncertain, an illusion brought about by the promise of success.

Interlude Number Nine

(The following poem by Katrina Van Tassel appeared in the Dudley Farm Newsletter Farm News, Summer, 1999. In it she uses the allegory of pruning for benefits of change).

Pruning

Cutting back is vital to a clear view
To go about the job I take shears in hand
Blades must be keen, the clipping neat
I move from here to there
selecting what I no longer need,
what blocks my view of things
Outlook must be preserved
I cut away aging brush, dead wood,
make room for new
allow light where needed
I hack out the stranglehold of climbers,
creepers, inhibitors of blossom
The discard pile heightens,
the outlook widens
Sunlight streams through like
sudden understanding
Discard will go to flame
the rest to compost's riches
I, tiller of gardens, bared to elements
Will dance with enlightenment

Chapter Ten

Manifestations

Every great work, every great accomplishment,
has been brought into manifestation through holding to the vision...
— FLORENCE SCOVEL SHINN

When Erastus Dudley died on June 11th, 1872, he must have been one of the wealthiest citizens of North Guilford. Well respected, he had achieved a level of success in his long life that had eluded his father and left a legacy that continues to live on into the 21st century. The Dudley family faced the future financially secure with the resources and means necessary to bring them confidently through the next 120 years. As time would reveal, the greatest manifestation of that success would be the Dudley Farm Erastus created and sold to his son Nathan in 1864.

The 1870 U.S. Census listed 87 year old Erastus as a retired farmer and merchant. He owned real estate valued at $4300.00 and had a personal estate of over $30,000.00. The bulk of this estate was in U.S. Government Bonds, railroad stocks, and savings in ten different bank accounts.[1] Erastus had sold his home and farm to son Nathan C. Dudley in 1864 so the Dudley Farm was not among the properties listed in the census. In that sale, Nathan had purchased for $2500.00, 107 acres that included the house and other buildings as well as the horse barn across the Durham Road.[2] Of all the Dudley's listed in the 1870 census, Erastus is the only one that shows an increase in the total value of his property, that of all his sons had declined.

133

In his will Erastus provided for most of his surviving children as recorded in the Guilford Probate Records.[3] He mentions four of his surviving sons by name but does not mention his 58 year old son Luther F., who would die four years later in a wagon accident. Luther it may be recalled, was the son who received a house for "consideration of love and good will and service" in the 1830's and seemed to be the lead brother in regard to the tannery operation. Was his exclusion a reflection of the squabble over the closing of the tannery as alluded to in family lore? His oldest son James, by then 64, is included however and it may be recalled, for whom, no other records exist. My guess is that he must have moved from the area long ago but was included in the will having remained in the good graces of his father. The omission of Luther and the inclusion of James does raise some curious questions.

James, Erastus F., Ebenezer, and Nathan are directed by the will to divide their father's estate equally among themselves. The inventory of the estate recorded land holdings valued at $4300.00. Though substantial enough, the value of the land holdings is eclipsed by the personal estate in 1872 listed at well over $40,000.00. This makes the omission of Luther even more interesting in that with an estate of this size, exclusion carried a heavy financial penalty. The personal estate was listed as follows:

46 Shares National Bank	$6716.00
45 Shares Liberty Bank	$5580.00
15 Shares National Bank	$1365.00
20 Shares Merchant's Bank	$1860.00
Townsend Savings Bank	$ 702.00
Townsend Savings Bank	$2327.00
Connecticut Savings Bank	$2486.00
New Haven Savings Bank	$2878.00
National Savings Bank	$ 247.00
Middletown Savings Bank	$3915.00

Why so many accounts in so many different banks? By our standards it does seem a bit odd, but by following a common practice of his time, Erastus must have felt much safer with his investments and cash safely deposited in multiple accounts and banks. During the 19th century, banks notoriously and often failed, sometimes without warning when their assets and deposits could not cover their financial commitments or demands from depositors. There were no bank regulations in a true sense nor protection or insurance for depositors. Mr. Dudley, like many others, must have known it to be prudent to protect his money by putting it in multiple institutions and accounts.

Each of the four sons inherited over $1000.00 worth of property from their father and roughly $10,000.00 of bank assets, bonds, and stocks. When combined with their own assets, each was now in a strong financial position which would in turn benefit their families. Nathan, already owner of the 107 acre farm, was now financially secure. Probate records also reveal that 38 individuals owed Erastus money through his loaning practices and exactly how those accounts were settled is unknown though his sons must have benefited from their settlement as well. Mentioned in the will are a number of special items; son Ebenezer received an additional $50.00, his grandson William was given $500.00, and granddaughter Mary his carriage.

Erastus left to his daughters, none mentioned by name, and their husbands the bulk of his personal belongings to be divided up equally among them. The list included his clothing, some furniture, books, and some tools. So what would a gentleman of the 19th century leave behind? It's fun to take a look. For clothing, Erastus left:

Hat	Lap Coat
Overcoat	Dress Coat
Sack Coat	Jacket
Velvet Vest	1 Red Flannel Wrap
1 pr of Slippers	1 pr Cotton Stockings
4 Old Stockings	1 pr of Pants
Cotton Pants	Black/Olive Necktie
Cotton Necktie	3 Pocket Handkerchiefs (?)
2 Cotton Shirts	4 Cotton/Flannel Shirts
4 Old Shirts	4 pr of Drawers
1 Wool Stocking	1 pr Rubber Boots
1 pr Shoes	1 pr Slippers

Looked at from today, his wardrobe was quite scant. But for a frugal Yankee farmer, Erastus possessed more than enough and the list makes for an interesting glimpse at the material culture of the time.

As for furniture and household items, Erastus left very little since most of the items in the house more than likely went to Nathan back in 1864 or had been given away prior to his death. He did leave:

1 Arm Chair	Bed Quilt
1 Comforter	New Wool Cloth
White Flannel Blanket	2 Old Cotton Sheets
Colored Blanket	Pr of Flannel Sheets, Old
3 Cotton Sheets	4 Pillow Cases
1 Chest	

Erastus also left 5 books: a *Great Bible*, a *Large Bible*, a volume of *Abbot's History of the War*, a volume entitled *The Life of Christ*, and one called *History of Indians*. In the inventory tools and equipment associated with farming are listed along with an ox cart and carriage.[4] Shoe making tools were listed as well which interestingly connects Erastus to the early tannery days. Their existence reveals that not only did he build and operate the tannery; he also must have participated in the cottage industry of local shoe making.

With the death of Erastus, the Dudley Farm entered a new phase in its existence. During the next 40 years, the farm of today took shape and it is comforting to realize that the house, barns, and landscape would be readily recognized by Nathan and his family. During my tenure as museum curator at the Dudley Farm, I designed a self-guided tour of the farm buildings and grounds used by visitors. The tour includes the buildings still standing and those that have been removed prior to or since the creation of the museum. The self-guided tour allows visitors to experience the farm much as Nathan would have known it along with a few new additions added by the Dudley Foundation.

The tour begins with the Dudley House, then moves on to the workshop/shed directly behind it. From there the visitor is able to amble about the farm, taking in the three gardens; the herb and flower gardens, and the Heritage Garden. Created in the late 1990's on the exact location where David, and before him his mother, grandmother, and great grandmother had the family vegetable gardens, the Heritage Garden grows a number of heirloom varieties of vegetables that would have been found on a 19th century New England farm. As guests continue their tour, they are drawn magnetically to the old gray barn which dominates the property. Still used for the storage of hay in its lofts, the barn has stalls for horses and cattle and a milking area for cows. It also houses period farm equipment and tools as well as a small workshop for their maintenance.

Behind the older section of the Main Barn is the Sleigh Shed that was added by the Dudley's to house their sleighs and grain and storage sheds to the east that form a "U" shape off the main barn, creating a barnyard for the penning of livestock. Today the barnyard houses the small flock of farm sheep. To the east of the barn complex in a grove of trees the visitor can see the farm outhouse, a family size three seater, and the stone and cement foundation that once held a hen house. To the north are the fenced pastures where the farm's oxen can usually be found and back towards the house the rusting metal tower for the windmill that once pumped water from the Mennuckatuck River to the cistern below it.

Walking east where a new blacksmith shop stands is the site of the old wagon shed that was dismantled in the mid 1990's for safety reasons. This building once housed farm wagons, had a stable for oxen, and a small room for a hired farm hand. Before it was dismantled, the room still contained a bunk, a rusted wood stove, and parts of the wall had been covered with newspaper to block the winter wind. Hopefully someday it will be rebuilt. Behind the early 20th century tractor shed that was converted into the farm school house and workshop, is the foundation to an ice house that once stood on the property. The Dudley's had harvested ice each winter on a pond they created by damming a small stream that ran through what is now woods to the east. The remnants of the earthen dam are still visible. On the way to the dam site, visitors pass the rebuilt sugar house and the lower field that is home to the Community Garden.

The new buildings constructed on the farm surely would have been welcomed by the Dudley's and include the Munger Barn, a wagon and storage barn, a new hen house, and a series of small sheds to house livestock while in the pastures. Though the land today is much more forested than when Nathan walked it, the ten remaining acres of his original 107 still depict a strong sense of another time; a farm from an era lost to memory but surviving as a manifestation of what was once at the corner of the Durham Road and the old Fair Haven Turnpike.

As a gentleman farmer of status and means, Nathan engaged in farming in a different way than his predecessors, participating in the new modern agricultural practices of the late 19th century. He belonged to a group of regional men who discussed the latest scientific developments on a regular basis to determine the best practices to increase crop yields, milk production, and general improvements in animal husbandry. As a result, Nathan was possibly the first area farmer to introduce Holstein cows, a superior milk producer whose iconic black and white coloring would come to symbolize the dairy cow for the next century. Thus by the 1880's, life on the Dudley's farm would have fallen into a comfortable routine determined by the seasons and the continuous rhythms of farm life. Even as drastic economic change was sweeping through North Guilford, transforming it forever, Nathan's farm remained an island of constancy protected by the legacy of his father and his own innovative farming practices.

Comfortable and complacent would not have been two words used to describe the Dudley Foundation and its plans for the farm in 1999. Moving dynamically forward we had worked hard during the winter to hit the ground running in the spring with a new operational design triggered by Doug Williamson's resignation and a new optimism brought to the farm by the addition of the Barrows property. Thanks to work done at the Barrows house led per usual by Henry and Bob, along with Joan Stettbacher and many volunteers, it was ready for a tenant that spring. Joan, never one to shy away from a difficult task, had taken on the responsibility of supervising the property and repairs as well as securing a tenant. With a renter secured, we turned our attention to the Dudley Farm itself.

At meetings the previous fall and all during the winter the board of directors, along with a number of Foundation members who routinely attended them, hammered out a new plan to operate the farm. It was decided that I should take on the role of curator due to my history and archeology background, and that a new position of Development Director should be created to oversee fund raising and events. As curator, my job would be to organize the farm's collection of hundreds of artifacts donated over the years and get them, along with the buildings, up to museum standards. I would also put together displays and oversee our volunteer docents. Newcomer to the Foundation, North Guilford native Kristie Rubendunst, became the new tenant in the apartment on the north side of the farm house and the Director of Development. Another attempt at creating committees to meet the expanding needs of the farm began along with an appeal to members to join them if they could. The six committees, headed up by board or foundation members, were Museum, Buildings and Grounds, Fund Raising, Events, Education, and Land Use. The Land Use committee would act as an umbrella for vital sub committees that included the Farmer's Market, the Farm Co-op, the Flower, Herb, and later Heritage Gardens, the Community Garden, and Livestock. We were ready.

That February Tom and I, with the assistance of the independent study students, tapped the farm's maples, boiled the sap to syrup in the rebuilt Sugar House, and filled small bottles for sale at the farm. We also hosted hundreds of local and regional students who participated in and learned about old time maple sugaring. It was a great success and as curator, I even ran a program one cold Saturday attended by close to 100 hardy visitors curious to see how it was all done. We continued to welcome students the rest of the year through the *Back to the Future* program and by the end of June had helped over 4000 eager young faces experience the farm.

The Farmer's Market continued to grow that year with more vendors and customers each Saturday as word spread throughout Guilford and neighboring towns. Through the work of the Farm Co-op members, the farm received certification from the Northeast Organic Farmers Association as an organic farm, a milestone in our attempt to preserve the rich agricultural heritage of the region. Finally, to make the farm truly complete, resident livestock and chickens were added, bringing it to life through their presence in a way nothing else could. The barnyard and newly fenced pastures were now home to a small but growing flock of Corriedale and Hampshire sheep, Nubian goats, and the two Shorthorn oxen, Nate and Lu. Nate and Lu came to the farm as young calves and under the steady hand of Mark Dudley and his son

Evan, had begun the long process of learning to work as a team. Board member Janet and her husband Mark, both very distant relatives of the farm's Dudley's, brought the sheep and oxen to the farm and in return would care for them and the rest of the livestock including the chickens. A new chicken house and yard was constructed to house the flock of hens and a rooster. The Dudley Farm had become a real living farm for the first time in 40 years.

Kristie dove into her role as Director of Development with gusto and enthusiasm. A font of new ideas, she quickly organized what became known as the Friday Night Series at the farm. Designed to bring members and others to the farm on a regular basis, create publicity, and help bring in new members and donations, events were planned for the first three Fridays of each month. The first Friday evening hosted local and regional musicians who performed in the intimate setting of the dining room and parlor of the house. This venue ranged from classical to traditional and folk and quickly drew a dedicated group to the farm to experience the farm and the charming atmosphere created by the music. Within a matter of months a group of local traditional musicians were so inspired by the farm as a setting for their music they organized a Saturday jam session often attended by as many as 25 musicians and twice that number of spectators who would gather to tap their toes to the sounds of a forgotten era. It was an experience.

The second Friday was devoted to poetry. Presented in conjunction with the *Guilford Poets Guild*, local poets gathered under the leadership of Katrina Van Tassel to share their work and experience the joy and beauty of what each had to offer. By the late spring, so many devotees to the art were gathering each Friday the venue was forced to move from the cozy confines of the house to the outdoor area behind the great gray barn. The third Friday each month was devoted to history topics and discussions. I had the pleasure of giving talks a number of times and the idea that this event soon became an opportunity for people in the community to learn more about local history was a popular one. Building on the farm's past successes, Kristie organized events and workshops throughout the year including the annual Farm Day that had grown out of the original fire company open houses.

Energy and excitement had been rekindled at the farm and for the first time in a long while there was very little dissention on the board, replaced with a feeling of satisfaction tempered by the knowledge that we still needed to move forward. Fortified by a new sense of purpose, the board began reaching out in earnest to the business community of Guilford with a mixed degree of success, yet our renewed confidence as an organization was noted which would prove beneficial in the future. If nothing else, the Dudley Farm was now recognized as an established and viable institution within the community.

That summer the Dudley Farm received the area Citizen of the Year award from the local Totoket Grange. In existence since the 1890's, the Grange each year recognized a person, group, or organization that in some way made a positive contribution or difference within the communities it served; Guilford, Branford, and North Branford. Doug and I accepted the award for the farm and together spoke of how important the recognition of the Grange meant to us as an organization. Established to advance the cause of local agriculture, this century old institution, by acknowledging the Dudley Farm and its efforts to preserve local agricultural history, had marked us with a legitimacy no other group could.

Back at the farm, it did not take long to feel the positive energy born of confidence and success. Events were packed, the Farmer's Market was booming, and the farm was becoming for many in North Guilford and beyond a community center and resource long envisioned back in the early days. A new roof was put on the main barn, a visible sign to all of our progress, Jerri Guagdano and her business partner, Mary Pacelli had completed replacing the wall paper on the bottom floor of the house, membership was up, and the Saturday docents Shirley Gonzalez and Irene Ayers were at times overwhelmed with giving tours of the house. It was really more than we could all have hoped for and a rewarding harvest due to the hard work and determination of so many members and volunteers. Not only had the Dudley Farm been saved, it was thriving.

During the last three decades of the 19th century, the Dudley Farm also thrived amidst an atmosphere of contented and comfortable complacency. That would not have been the case however, for the majority of their neighbors in North Guilford. The last decades of the 1800's were cruel ones for most small farming communities as Connecticut and surrounding states continued their rush towards industrialization and urbanization. Rural residents abandoned their farms in increasing numbers for the steady pay check factories offered and young people left the farm to the older generations to pursue the American dream in new and exciting ways. In New Haven and Meriden, Bridgeport and Waterbury, they mingled with the flood of European immigrants who came for the same reasons, turning their backs on the traditional lifestyle and values of the past. Cities were alive with seductive promise, alluring in their energy and excitement, and full of the future. Back on the farm, tradition still reigned alongside financial hardship and diminished expectations.

Yet on the Dudley Farm, cushioned by inheritance and pragmatic farming, many of the dynamic forces bringing change to their neighbors were kept at bay. Nathan and his family would certainly have lamented the impact on neighbors and friends and must have cast a wary eye as more and more land began the slow process of reforestation as fields turned to brush and homes were left to the elements. The big white house on the gentle rise must have appeared a beacon of stability in a sea of change.

In 1880, Nathan's son Erastus was 31 years old and as the only son, heir to the family farm. Working alongside his 69 year old father, he must have taken over most of the responsibility for the day to day operation and work on the 107 acres. Erastus had married Martha Crowell Munger (1854-1931) from the northern part of the neighboring town of Madison in 1875 and in 1876 their daughter, Mabel was born. At some point after, the northern section of the house was added. Whether or not the marriage of Erastus and Martha led to that construction is not known, but when it was added, the family home was substantially altered. Besides Nathan and Sophronia, in 1880 it was still home to two of their daughters, Lucy and Mary and thus the house held two families and three generations. In 1881, son Nathan Chidsey was born adding one more to the four bedroom house.

The decision to add what was essentially a separate living area to the Dudley house reveals some interesting cultural differences that existed by then when compared to that of the three generation living arrangement evident when it was first built in the 1840's. Then there were a total of nine people, the seven members of Nathan's family plus his father and mother occupying the seven room, three bedroom home. The kitchen was the shared domain of both adult women, Ruth and Sophronia, and the three bedrooms and a later fourth more than accommodated the extended family of three generations. All were apparently comfortable with the shared space and by the standards of the time, lived in a less individualistic and more corporate environment where individuals did not require nor expect private space.

Changes in American society during the late 19ᵗʰ century resulted in a different use of space that corresponded with the growth of individuality in a more modern sense. The rise of an increasingly individualistic culture came with the development of a more industrialized and urbanized society that also encouraged the consumption of consumer goods and the display of material wealth. A sign of this change was an increase in the size of homes, rooms, and a new emphasis on display that became known as the Victorian style. Space within rooms became busy and crowded, especially those considered public such as parlors, dining rooms, and a new one called a sitting room, as they became stuffed with the signs of family wealth and affluence. Furniture became more opulent and formal as overstuffed horse hair settees replaced simple chairs, wall paper more striking, colorful, and bold, and draperies and curtains heavier and more ornate.

At the same time, especially in the expanding cities, people became more alienated from others as the sheer scale and size of the population grew. Unlike North Guilford, where everyone knew one another, their families, and their histories, in the new urban landscapes most of those encountered were strangers and unfamiliarity bred an increased insecurity that for some fed a need to surround oneself with the material trappings of success that gave one a sense of purpose and identity. This new urban and material culture, fed by a cash economy and growing disposable incomes, found its way into rural communities where those of means mimicked and embraced it as a way of differentiating themselves from their less affluent neighbors, especially as the economic conditions within those communities continued to deteriorate. Larger houses, more rooms, and greater amounts of personal space became for those who could, the norm. The Dudley's could.

Neighbors and friends were coming to stare in wonder. Would it fall? How can those sticks hold the weight? What if the wind blows? The new section of the house was being built using a technique not yet seen much in North Guilford and certainly not along the increasingly busy Durham Road. Called a balloon frame, it looked precariously fragile compared to the solid timber frame that houses had always been constructed. Erastus had worried as well as the carpenter, a distant cousin of his from Guilford village, began putting the first of the walls together as they lay on the newly decked foundation. "William, you will assure me it will stand?" he asked nervously as the first flimsy wall frame, made of two inch by six inch milled studs held together by nails, was raised and braced to the deck so as to not fall.

"Erastus" he reminded him, "the strength will come with all sides attached and the second floor laid. Your home will be as sound and as strong as the old for each part binds the other to form a stout whole."

Erastus remembered the house down on Fair Street he had watched William build the autumn past, quickly raised as if through magic, each wall bracing the other to form the "balloon". He had noted how timely and economically it had been constructed, an attractive argument when he had spoken to his father of the need to expand the family home.

At first Nathan had been hesitant; balking at the idea and the cost that a timber frame entailed but was curious when told of the reduced cost of the new framing technique. "The cost might merit a look" he had cautioned. Curiosity in the end did get the best of him, especially after he had watched the progress of another Fair Street house himself. Now Nathan called himself a true believer. But he still questioned the need for "a frivolous luxury" as he called the addition. "Son, I know the times have changed and recognize the need for your family, but it is the separate kitchen that I believe warrants it," acknowledging that though amicable, relations between his wife and Martha were not always sound. "Two strong women can sometimes ruin a good stew" he recalled his grandmother saying. "Perhaps for peace in the house this is best."

For Martha, it was a Godsend. Though she cared for her mother-in-law, there were times when their relationship was difficult, especially when she constantly questioned how she raised Mabel and young Nate. "She is stuck in the past and does not rule me or my children" Martha had exclaimed through tears one evening. "Erastus, we must find our own home."

"Out of the question" had been his response, "for this farm is our future and our children's as well." That is when the idea sprang to him; "we can

*build our own home right here by adding a section, creating an even grander
structure and giving all the space they require." "Besides" he explained as he
wove together his thoughts, "it will serve us all well and be a testimony to the
prosperity we now enjoy."*

*Even his mother came around to the idea and she and Martha became
fast friends with the anticipation of space and compromise pending. The
reality was, they both agreed, they were too much alike.*

*As the grand addition neared completion, Nathan and Sophronia
broached an idea one evening as dinner was ending. "Perhaps the space in
this old house would better serve your needs as a family" Nathan half stated
and asked.*

*"The new end is smaller and may be more suitable to our requirements
for the kitchen here is larger and the farm office bares consideration."*

*"And my dear" Sophronia added as she turned to Martha, "there is also
space here for more children which would truly please us all."*

*With that the decision was made, Erastus and Martha would remain
in the grand but older part of the home and Nathan and Sophronia would
reside in the new.*

The addition to the north side expanded the living space in the house by
close to fifty percent. Built in the Greek Revival style to match the rest,
the gable end was turned towards the Durham Road to form an "ell"
shape. Two stories tall, the new section contained a large kitchen and
parlor on the bottom floor and three bedrooms on the second. Like the
original section of the house, it also included a walk-up attic. Though
now a separate unit joined only by a door between the two kitchens,
when first built it was much more integrated into the main house. On
the first floor, the front parlor was joined with the left side parlor of
the original house, now the farm library, by double doors that could be
opened to make a larger space for family gatherings and entertaining.
Both parts of the house were also connected with a door between the
kitchens, a door between two adjacent bedrooms in the front, and a
door that once connected a corridor to the rear on the upper floor.

In its entirety, the Dudley house became imposing in its scale and
design. The addition still gives it a looming quality as it raises itself
above the road, exaggerated by the fine example of the temple-like pediment in the gable. Many older homes during the late 19th and early 20th

centuries were altered and expanded during this time and most combined more modern Victorian or Gothic styles with an older form. Not so the Dudley's, they meticulously stayed with the style of the original, creating an image of stability and permanence as if to say "we are still here, and will continue so", a remarkable statement of how Nathan and his son Erastus saw themselves, their heritage, and the family future. Of note, exactly when the addition was added is still unclear but probably at some point during a 30 year window between 1880 and 1910.

As previously mentioned, the Dudley Farm of today is a manifestation of this period. In shape and form, the house, outbuildings, and landscape would change little over the next 100 years making it the historic treasure it is. Apparently, by the time Nathan died in 1912 and his son Erastus followed him in 1919, there was little reason or motivation to make changes and the farm consequently fell into a comfortable slumber of permanence.

Interlude Number Ten

(The following essay appeared in the Curator's Corner section of the Dudley Farm Newsletter Farm News, Winter/Spring 2004. In it I wrote about the process involved in making sure the Dudley Farm, as a museum, depicted the past as accurately as possible. The goal: that Nathan C. Dudley would recognize it as home.)

What comes to mind when you think about the past? Do you focus on a person, a place, an event, or a particular time? We all have our own sense of the way life may have been which is shaped by our experiences and interests, the books we have read, the stories we have heard, and the movies and television we have seen. But how do we sort out fact from fancy, reality from myth? It's easy to create in our own minds what we'd like the past to be—but is it real and is it important to be so?

Imagine being given the gift of time travel. As you journeyed back through time would you be surprised by the sights, sounds, and smells? What would it be like to talk to people whose lives were so different than your own? What questions would you ask? Then, what would happen when you returned to our time—would your stories and descriptions be believed? One thing would be certain, the facts you brought back would have to speak for themselves and the past would live through them.

In many ways, the Dudley Farm is a time machine that allows us all to make that journey to the past; to see, hear, and smell another time. The work of creating that past however, is far from perfect. As an organization, The Dudley Foundation has sought to bring the farm back to a facsimile of what it might have been around the year 1900 aided by photographs, research, stories, and conjecture. What has been created and restored to date is a reflection of those many successes and occasional mistakes.

The importance of doing things correctly in reflecting the past as a museum is and should be the primary concern of the Dudley Foundation. Whether it is in restoring buildings, gardens, or the grounds, attention has and must continue to be paid to what is an accurate portrayal of the farm in the late 19th century. Progress can be and has been slow at times, but the price of not being careful would be to deny the past and the ability of future generations to experience it. It would discredit the Dudley Farm as a museum.

We have been given a wonderful opportunity to assist one another in creating a window into another time at a place where nothing of historic importance happened other than the fact that ordinary men, women, and children lived out their lives and dreams for three hundred years there. Our efforts are a testimony to their struggles and triumphs and give meaning to their lives. Our efforts are also a gift to those in future years who will visit the Dudley Farm to learn of and experience those past lives. We owe it to all of them to try and get things right.

We'd like to think that if Nathan Dudley, the patriarch of the Dudley family during the late 19th century, came for a visit home today he'd find much that was familiar. It would be fun to listen to his comments as to what was correct and what needed to be changed. And as Nathan told us the story of his time, we would be able to learn firsthand how things really were. Unfortunately, we will never speak to Nathan. But, we can and must rely upon our best efforts as if we could. Creating a past that Nathan would appreciate and understand to our utmost ability is the continuing goal of the Dudley Foundation and with your support that effort will continue. Together, let's make the farm a place Nathan would call home.

Chapter Eleven

Looking Forward

Every tomorrow has two handles. We can take hold of it
with the handle of anxiety or the handle of faith.
— HENRY WARD BEECHER

As the 20th century ended, the Dudley Foundation was in a
much better place than could have been imagined in those early years. Despite setbacks and squabbles, we had managed to
defy the odds and create a viable, living, and growing historical resource.
The anxiety that often typified the past years had been replaced with a
renewed feeling that the farm was on the right path and that the future
looked promising. We had grasped the handle of faith in our mission
and plunged into the new century with optimism and determination
much as the Dudley's might have 100 years before.

An integral part of that future was the Munger Barn. Long a project deferred, it sat for years tucked inside the rotting green container
truck on the farm, an alien 20th century intrusion behind the stone wall
along the path on the way to the sugar house. For visitors, the question
invariably arose—"so what's in the trailer?" By the winter of 2000, some
on the board had grown tired of answering and knew it was time to
move forward. It wasn't long before a whole new slew of questions and
challenges emerged once we opened those hulking metal doors of the
trailer. What condition was the frame that had been so carefully dismantled? Once removed from storage, what would be usable and what
would not? What about the design for the barn's use; who would do

that and how would it reflect the historic nature of the structure while servicing the needs of the Dudley Farm? What would the old barn's use actually be and how would it mesh with the mission of the Foundation? Who would do the work and the inevitable elephant in the room—how would it all be paid for?

Meetings that winter and spring soon took on the air of those early days when the farm was more a dream than a reality. Was the Munger Barn really necessary? If it was, how would we use it? How would we pay for it and how might this graying but still feisty group that had so long guided the farm find the energy to bring it back to life? Once again, the dining room to the farm house where weekly meetings were held became the scene of heated debate as each question was tackled with the furious emotion of a good family argument. In the end it came down to two issues—design and money.

As that winter turned to spring and the debates wound to an end, it was determined that the barn's new life would be that of a multi-use facility, one that could accommodate museum displays, a possible office, storage, and most importantly space for gatherings, meetings, and classes. The barn might also become a source of income for the farm as rental space for weddings and events. Doug dove into the design phase with his usual passion, bringing back to each meeting reworked plans for the barn, slowly transforming on paper what we hoped would stand on the very spot where the crumbling stone foundation of the Dudley's original 18th century barn still stood. As he and Henry took on the role of co-chairs of the Munger Barn committee, all the minute details that bring a modern building to life became clearer—and more expensive. By that summer, the frame still sat in its rusting home, surrounded by weeds and Queen Anne's lace, still eliciting the perpetual question about its existence.

Then there was the perpetual bane of all non-profits: money. No single issue had in the past caused such divisive acrimony within the foundation's board and the Munger Barn proved no exception. The reality was simple, though we now were able to meet our monthly expenses, a project of this size would require capital beyond the scope of the farm's income. Estimated to cost a minimum of $150,000, the Munger Barn project would propel us into the type of fund raising arena none on the board felt comfortable with on either a personal or institutional level. Without a specific and detailed plan for design and cost, it would also be impossible to secure a loan, something the more fiscally conservative members of the board were adamantly against. As the task became more daunting, so did the question: was this really necessary? Old arguments returned; were we over-reaching again, some felt, as in the case of the Barrow's Farm? Where was this leading us? Did we really want the farm to grow? Would this put the entire farm in jeopardy? Like the Dudley's in 1900, we were faced with the security of complacency or the uncertainty that risk might bring. Which would be the best for the future well-being of the farm? We needed to have faith in our decision.

In February, 1890, the family surprised 69 year old Nathan with a birthday celebration. The wind was howling that blustery cold day as he walked in from the barn, having spent the bulk of the day grooming his two prized trotters, horses he loved to hitch to his carriage in the fine weather of summer and his sleigh when the snows covered the Durham Road and he could feel a young man again; the cold wind rushing past his face turning it as bright as a lantern. "Old man" scolded Sophronia, "I was about to send young Nate to the stalls to see if you had frozen yourself solid. If only you paid me the attention you give those two black devils".

"They do not nag a man as you do and for that I am grateful" Nathan returned as he held his cold hands to her cheeks, a gesture of his that she had long since given in to as inevitable.

The kitchen was warm and their side of the house quiet, maybe too so he thought. "What are they all about" Nathan queried his wife. "For a late Sunday afternoon is never so with Mabel about".

At age 14, his granddaughter always brought with her presence a storm of commotion and energy that he found delightful if at times tiring. "I do believe she is in the front parlor by the stove, complaining of her grandfather's inattention" Sophronia chided.

"Well, I'll see to that" he declared as he walked into their section of the two joined parlors of the big house, to the delighted cheers of his family and friends.

When we were setting up the second floor of the Dudley house as a museum in the mid 1990's, one of the enjoyable discussions was how each of the four bedrooms should be represented. In the front corner room it was decided to set up the old loom to demonstrate rag rug making, leaving the two rooms to the rear of the house and the front middle room as bedrooms. The front one to the north of the staircase was set up as an adult bedroom with a full size bed and donated furniture that would depict the room of Nathan and Sophronia or their son Erastus and his wife Martha. Of the two rear rooms, the larger over the dining room was shown to be both a bedroom and a multi-purpose storage area typical of homes in the 19th century. Here are displayed, besides a rope bed, various pieces of equipment associated with wool processing; a great wheel for spinning, a flax wheel for linen, and other long forgotten items used in the processing of wool and linen fabric at home. Though equipment not used by the late 19th century, we felt it was important to display these vital tools of the past. Theirs is a story of home processing and self-reliance, when store bought was an expensive option beyond the reach of the average farm family until the time of the Industrial Revolution.

The entire upstairs as well as the stairwell leading up from the porch in the front of the house were cleaned and painted by a number of farm and board member volunteers that made their final set up as representations of the past possible. Even though the peeling wall paper had been removed in the early 1990's, every room on the second floor was showing its age. Thanks to the efforts of farm members Ted Tichy, Bill Barnes, Evelynne Tichy, Linda Curry, and Lorraine Ashman, this section of the house was restored to reflect the late 19th century with the plaster walls patched and painted and cleaned for the first time in decades. Due to their efforts, it was a pleasure as curator to begin the process of depicting those rooms as they might have appeared in 1900. The stairwell in particular was brought back to life as a center piece of the Dudley home through the hard work of Ted, Bill, Henry, and the paper hanging skills of Jerri Guadagno and Mary Pacelli.

As for the little bedroom above the farm office, it was decide it would belong to Mabel. Mabel Dudley Rossiter was an interesting reflection of how changing times were shaping life not just for the Dudley family, but also life in North Guilford by the beginning of the 20th century. A unique personality, Mabel was a graduate of Mount Holyoke College, something unusual for the time when few women attended college and even fewer from a small rural community like North Guilford did so. This speaks volumes of the status of the Dudley family and how they saw themselves in relation to the greater society when only the more affluent would deem female education beyond the local public school important or necessary. Oral tradition describes Mabel as a free-thinking spirit, creative and fun loving and as a result one of North Guilford's more interesting residents. A botanist, artist, and humanitarian, Mabel married Francis Rossiter and spent the rest of her life in the community of her birth. In the Fall 2000 *Farm News*, I included a description of Mabel by her son, life-long North Guilford resident Morris Rossiter who had sent it in a letter to his friend and Dudley Farm member Carol Usher. It captures her personality and character nicely. In it, Morris wrote:

> She did attend Mount Holyoke College and perhaps there developed a sense of public service. For years she collected worn but serviceable clothing and sent it at her own expense to the Tuskegee Institute in Alabama. She was ahead of her time on race relations.
>
> The family bought a Willies-Knight car in 1922. Although Francis learned to drive, he was more interested in horses so Mabel did the driving, probably the first woman in North Guilford to do so.

Morris then continued with this story:

> Mabel was always active in church. She was a life-long member of the choir and served for many years, not for the honor certainly, but because of a sense of duty. Mabel was also the unofficial decorator of the church. This brought out her most glaring weakness… tardiness. The congregation would start to be seated when Mabel arrived with a profusion of flowers. With complete unconcern she would arrange things just so even if the minister had taken his place and occasionally peer down to see how things were going. This routine was a great embarrassment to her children.

The final description was of Mabel's adventures with the Branford Garden Club.

> Because Guilford did not have a garden club at the time, Mabel joined the Branford Garden Club. She was only interested in flowers and the social aspect of the club escaped her. Early one spring, a famous flower arranger gave a lecture in New Haven and invited attendees to bring in arrangements to be critiqued. Mabel invited a cousin Blanche from North Branford to ride in with her. Blanche, who liked to know what was going on, inquired what Mabel was submitting and was told briskly "potato sprouts and skunk cabbage". Blanche sniffed a little feeling that she had been put on. However, the arrangement sure enough consisted of a piece of rotted log, some moss, potato sprouts (which after a winter in the cellar had grown to over a foot and a half long and were pearly white) and some early buds of skunk cabbage which of course were quite colorful... plus some other items long since forgotten.
>
> When the lecturer came to Mabel's arrangement, she stepped back and said "it's perfect! I wouldn't change a thing". It was the only arrangement to receive such an accolade. Afterwards, Mabel, who was not much given to bragging, did observe with a trace of a smile that Blanche was awfully quiet on the ride home.[1]

Not only did Mabel have an eye for flower arranging, she also was a rather accomplished artist. Gracing her bedroom at the back of the Dudley house is a colorful and evocative painting she did of North Guilford's Lake Quonnipaug. Set near the window in the room that affords one a picturesque look at the gardens, fields, and woodland of the farm, the two views together remind the visitor of that world the Dudley Foundation has worked so hard to save and Mabel must have loved.

In 1900, the Dudley house was home to five family members making up three generations; 79 year old Nathan, Erastus and Martha, 51 and 46 respectively, 24 year old Mabel and her brother Nathan C., 19. Sophronia had died in 1890 at the age of 68 leaving her husband, the family patriarch, to carry on as best he could. Her loss undoubtedly created pallor over the stately home, as Nathan occupied the newer addition alone. In 1904, his grandson Nathan married Amy Dudley (1878-1967), a distant cousin, and soon the house sprang to life with all the commotion and energy the newlyweds must have brought with them, no doubt to the great pleasure of the old gentleman. Yet under the veneer of excitement and anticipation the family surely felt as the young couple established a section of the house as their home, the realities of farm life in the early 20th century must have begun to take hold, creating an underlying anxiety for the future.

The responsibility for the farm by 1904 was certainly shared by 55 year old Erastus and young Nathan who together faced the yearly challenge of trying to keep it economically viable. Along with staples of corn and hay, dairy farming had been added though on a small scale by today's standard with perhaps one to two dozen cows. Maple syrup production began along with continued ice production. During the second half of the 19th century, maple sugar had been replaced by processed cane sugar from the American South and the Caribbean in most New England households and enterprising farmers such as the Dudley's had switched from maple sugar to the production of syrup to supplement their income. Begun under the older Nathan, production had continued under Erastus, and later his son Nathan who sold it under the *Nathan C. Dudley and Sons* label. When asked for his earliest memory of his grandfather Erastus, Morris Rossiter replied in the fall/winter 2005 Farm News that it was when he was about two years old in 1918. Morris recalled, "I barely remember one passing memory being down in the sap house, sitting on Grandpa Dudley's lap".[2]

Work on the farm remained labor intensive as reflected in a rare personal account that has survived from the family at the time. In September 1897, when he was 16 years old, young Nathan Dudley wrote the following school essay on a day's farming. By the way, he received an A for his effort. Published in the July 2000 Farm News, Nathan described a day's effort haying.

When I speak of and describe a day's farming I do not say or by any means intend to say that any two days are alike as far as work is concerned. There is always variety and perhaps this makes the work more attractive than the routine of the city laborer.

About this time of year there are so many things to be done that it seems as if they will never end.

We do not consider 4 o'clock too early in the morning to begin the "chores", that is, to milk and turn the cows to pasture, the horses must be fed and curried; well there is always some odd job left over from the day before that can easily be done before breakfast which comes along about 6 o'clock.

After breakfast we are generally given the work to be done. Someone is sent to harness the horses and plow the ground for the next year's grain. This means weary miles of walking in the freshly moved soil, guiding the plow and horses and also keeping temper for no means is this pleasant work. There are meadows which have not been mowed because of the more important and valuable pieces of grass.

The scythes must be sharpened and when we are provided with long rubber boots we "start in". In such places as we go we are not surprised to often scare out snakes and turtles of different kinds. It is not pleasant to hear a slight hiss and see a snake glide from under your boot and make for his hole which is always near. Quite frequently a howl is heard from some unlucky person whose scythe or boot has demolished a hornet's nest and who is being made the subject of a vigorous attack by enraged insects

We are all very glad whatever we are doing to hear the call to dinner and are not long in getting home. After dinner if we are not wanted in the hay field there are acres and acres of corn to be cut up and stacked or if this is already done it has to be picked and carted to the barns. This is very pleasant work or would be if it were not for getting up and emptying our baskets so often.

Often we are set at work cleaning off the stones from the fresh plowed ground and this seems to be a never ending job. If we finish this there are pumpkins to gather and take to the barn, or apples to pick or, there is always something to do.

When chore time comes again we all quit work and by

seven o'clock are ready for supper. In the evening we can find plenty to do in running the corn sheller, mending harnesses, making axe handles for the coming winters use or if nothing better, sorting apples and other fruit.

We generally leave off work at about 10 o'clock because we must be rested for the next day's labor.[3]

From the letter we can gleam not only Nathan's pride in his work, but the sheer volume of what needed to be done at harvest time. Throughout his account, Nathan also refers to work being done as a group; at that vital time of the year, hired hands, neighboring boys, family, and friends all labored together to get the tasks done and the crops in. Much of what Nathan described had not changed in 200 years and his Dudley ancestors would have agreed that the life of a farmer was one of working together through long hours, hard work and collective necessity.

A walk today through the Dudley Farm property and into the woodland that makes up the Guilford Land Preservation Trust land to the Barrows Farm, collectively now known as the Dudley/Barrows Woods, is a walk through time and all the diversity that nature has to offer in the uplands that make up much of North Guilford. Winding through verdant wetlands, rocky outcrops, and majestic stands of oak, ash, and birch, the old farm roads that lead through the woods form a peaceful escape from the incessant drone of traffic on the two busy state roads to the west and south. Yet these tranquil acres also hold a secret to another source of income the Dudley's may have possibly enjoyed during the late 19th century and into the first two decades of the next: charcoal.

Charcoal making was a major industry in the belt of land extending about eight miles north of the Connecticut shoreline west to east from North Branford and North Guilford all the way to the Connecticut River to what is now the town of Deep River. These communities and those in between such as Killingworth shared a common landscape of hard scrabble fields and rocky outcrops left over from the glaciers 15,000 years ago. A tough area to farm, the leading commodity of these lands was timber for the first 200 years of European settlement. By the late 18th century, most of the timber had been cut and the denuded hills had become pasture for the sheep that became lucrative for those such as Erastus Dudley and his partners in their currying mill. As the agricultural fortunes of the region continued to decline by the mid 1800's, many of the more marginal farms were abandoned and the fields and meadows were left to begin the process of reforestation which continued throughout the 20th century. Covered by new growth forests of ash, birch, maple, and most importantly oak, these newly wooded fields supplied the wood that could be converted to charcoal to be burned in the insatiable furnaces of the late 19th century factories in surrounding cities and towns.

Charcoal making was a time consuming process and art that became the domain of itinerant colliers, as the charcoal makers were called, who moved from farm to farm and woodlot to woodlot throughout the area. Walter Landgraf, in his description of local charcoal making in nearby North Madison described the time consuming process. According to Landgraf, they created what were called piles, mounds of wood and earth that were fashioned into charcoal burning furnaces, that each consumed anywhere from 20 to 50 cords of wood. Done during the months of March and November, colliers would tend as many as 15 piles along with their assistants at a time. Once a pile had been constructed, a 10 to 14 day burn would follow, yielding between 30 and 40 bushels of charcoal which would then be allowed to cool before being loaded on wagons to be brought to a furnace or factory in the region.

Charcoal making was a ten step process from start to finish and took between 20 to 30 days. It started with the clearing and leveling of the burn or hearth area, 30[ft] to 40[ft] in diameter. Wood was then delivered to the hearth and organized by size and girth; pieces called billets that were 4 feet long and 4 to 7 inches in diameter and lap wood that were 4 feet long and 1½ to 4 inches in diameter. The next step was the placing of a fagan pole in the center of the hearth, a tall pole reaching to a height of 18 feet or so. Around the fagan pole a three sided lap wood chimney was constructed, a crib like structure built to a height of between 14[ft] and 18[ft] or the height of the pile to be made.

Around the lap wood chimney the pile was then built. Billets were placed in a circular sequence around the chimney, the closest row upright and the further out on an increasing angle. Lap wood was used to fill in any gaps as the pile was built as it grew to a diameter of 20 to 30 feet and a height of 14. The entire pile was next covered with leaves and ferns and then that layer was buried under a foot deep layer of finely sifted dirt. This dusting, as it was called, would allow for the control of air entering the pile as it burned; less meant more air, more meant less air. The pile was then lit by placing small pieces of wood into the chimney and fired with coals from a campfire. Once fired, it would take up to 14 days for the burn to reach the foot of the pile, in the process driving out all chemicals except carbon from the wood inside. During the burn, the collier and assistants would monitor the pace of the burn by reading the signs of the smoke, filling in low spots and tamping out high ones to control it. Once done, the pile was opened up and sections raked so they might air cool, which could take up to one week.[4]

While constructing the pile and monitoring it's burn, the collier would often build a small hut to live in, usually measuring 8ft x 10ft so as to be on the site 24 hours per day. Some itinerant colliers came with their own pre-fabricated shelter that could be set up and dismantled as they travelled from job to job. A dirty, smoky, and physically demanding process, charcoal making though profitable for the owner of the woodlot, was not something looked upon as acceptable work for farmers like the Dudley's, and in general the colliers and their assistants were probably looked upon with a bit of suspicion and mistrust. Thus the charcoal making process tended to be done at a distance from the farm if possible and back in the scruffy ridges and rocky woodlots most farmers owned. Doug Williamson has located a number of probable charcoal sites within the Dudley/Barrows Woods which might have been a prime location.

By the outbreak of World War I in 1914, charcoal making had pretty much run its course in the region. Just as the hills and ridges of Connecticut had once been stripped of their timber by the start of the 19th century, charcoal making had done the same to what had been left of the old growth and secondary growth forests. Replaced by coal from Pennsylvania, charcoal disappeared as an energy source allowing for the long process of 20th century reforestation in Connecticut to begin. For the Dudley's, this would have meant one less source of income.

In 1912, Nathan Dudley died at the age of 91 leaving his property to his son Erastus. Over his lifetime he had seen the complete transformation of the family farm and businesses from the early days of his father's work at the mill site, the rise and demise of the tannery, the building of the Dudley house and farm, and the late 19th century struggle to keep the farm viable. Nathan must have died knowing that he, from his father and through his son, were now passing on to his grandson and namesake a legacy of almost 100 years of toil and triumph over the economic forces that had driven so many other long established North Guilford families away and off the land. Yet I wonder if in those final days, as he stood on the porch of the house he had called home for 68 years, he worried about its future as he looked down the rise towards the Durham Road and towards the old mill site. Was he apprehensive or content? Did he have regrets or have faith in the decisions he, his son, and grandson had made? Clearly things had changed in North Guilford just as they had changed throughout the region. But the farm was still there, and with the fourth generation now gracing the home, there was no reason to doubt its future for in 1908, Nathan's great grandson Erastus Irwin (1908-1950) was born followed a year later by David (1909-1991). Just as his father Erastus had looked out with pride on what they had created together, now he, Nathan may have done the same, but was it through a vale of uncertainty?

In an interesting twist to the traditional pattern of land ownership as passed down from father to son, apparently Erastus, when he died seven years after his father, left in his will a portion of the farm property to his wife Martha. His will details that "... to Martha C. Dudley, widow, the life use of the following real estate as her dower , namely, the north part of the buildings included in the inventory of his estate, together with, when occupying the house, the joint use with Nathan C. Dudley..."[5] Perhaps he had not fully provided for the possibility of his death with a clearly stated will since the 70 year old Erastus may have felt longer years were in his future but at any rate, the ownership of the farm itself ended up shared. It was quickly passed on to Nathan however. In a transaction between mother and son, the 107 acres with buildings were sold to Nathan for $600, a small fraction of the value of the property.[6] Why that amount is anyone's guess, perhaps to cover some expenses Martha had incurred. In the document dated July 31, 1919, Martha sold the "homestead—100 and seven acres with buildings" and the "Tannery Lot—situated in Guilford along the Durham Turnpike opposite the homestead—4 acres". Of more interest however is the snap shot look the document gives us of the farm at that moment for in the transaction, it is outlined that both Martha and Nathan would have joint use of part of the property surrounding the house. It stated that there would be "Joint use of grounds between the front of the house and highway and a distance of 50^{ft} from the house on all sides, the well, woodshed east of the house, the water system, hen house, and yard southwest from the barn, a plot not exceeding ¼ of an acre in area not over 200^{ft} from the house for a vegetable garden".[7] Thus 65 year old Martha was assured use of all she would require until her death 12 years later.

What makes the transaction fun to look at besides the description of the farm is the light it sheds on the possible relationship between mother and son. By the standards of our day, one might react to the fact that Martha was insuring for herself the use of the garden and other resources on the farm and around the house for the rest of her life, something we might assume a son would allow his mother the use of without the need of a legal description and transaction. Was there friction between them or between son and father prior to his death? Why was the entire 100 plus acre farm and tannery lot not left to Nathan? We can only imagine.

By 1931, the year Martha died, North Guilford like the rest of Connecticut and the U.S. was mired in the depths of the Great Depression. The family and their farm, having survived the economic and innovative changes and upheavals that were part of the 1920's, now faced their most dire decade. Fifty year old Nathan certainly must have struggled to keep the farm out of the chaos with no doubt the help of his sons, Erwin 23 and David, 22 years old. But, with farm markets in tatters and no strong alternatives available, the Dudley's, like their neighbors must have turned to their own resources to survive, producing what food they needed and trying as best they could to sell or trade what they could in order to get by. Together, they struggled on.

The small dairy herd of 20 to 30 Holsteins was maintained well into the 1930's when new federal regulations covering milk production made the business less profitable for small producers. The remnants of this once important activity can still be seen at the farm today. A quick look into the main barn through the great sliding doors reveals the old milking area with its fading white paint, a requirement imposed by the government to promote more sanitary conditions in the dairy. The foundation for the milk house still remains in front of the barn to the right of the driveway where Nathan and his sons would store the milk to keep it cool until it was picked up by a wholesaler each day.

It does appear that the basic overall patterns of farm life established in the 1930's would dictate those on the farm for the next 30 years. Nathan continued to grow a variety of staples; grain, corn and hay and though he switched to a tractor and other mechanical equipment in the later decades of the 1940's and 50's, he always kept a team of draft horses which oral tradition says, he was quite proud of. Amy kept a traditional vegetable garden for the family food supply and also raised chickens, most notably, Rhode Island Reds. An ariel photograph taken in the 1940's shows a neat and well laid out Dudley farm which Nathan and Amy were no doubt quite proud of. Henry Tichy, who grew up just south of the farm on the Durham Road and worked for Nathan on the farm as a young boy, often recalled as we were restoring the farm how the house, barns, and grounds were always meticulously kept by the Dudley's and that Amy in particular kept the house and gardens, especially that of her prized gladioli, in pristine order.

What is now the Dudley Farm office in the small room behind the dining room was Nathans office as well and it was from there, as he sat by his old wooden roll-top desk, that he would manage the farm operation as best he could while also officiating as North Guilford's Justice of the Peace. Sharp witted and tongued, Nathan was a well-respected member of the North Guilford community and a man who in many ways lived in two centuries; in the traditions and practices of the 19th century and the realities of the 20th. Amy was the same, living in a world that harkened back to the past while doing her best with the present. Local residents still recall the sweetness and goodness that were part of her personality and the pride she had in her home which was often the scene of many North Guilford gatherings and get-togethers in the family dining room.

Together, Nathan, Amy, and their sons saw tremendous changes come to the area and the farm itself. Electricity came to North Guilford in the late 1920's and the house was electrified. Primitive and simple by today's standards, wiring for one light or outlet was eventually put into most rooms and can still be seen today. By far the biggest change to take place had to do with the land itself. Having inherited the 107 acres passed down through four generations, Nathan sold off most of it during his lifetime. By the time of his death in 1963, the Dudley's farm had shrunk to its present size of just over 10 acres. Like most of his farming neighbors, Nathan could not make ends meet farming on a regular basis and the best commodity available to sell and stay ahead was the farm itself. This unfortunate trend would continue for years throughout the region as farm after farm fell to the relentless demand for homes and development that would come to typify the second half of the 20th century. What thoughts might have gone through his mind as Dudley slowly sold off his livelihood and family legacy is unclear, but oral tradition describes him as becoming a bit callous and stern in later years, no doubt tempered by bitterness and regret.

One more shadow would fall across the farm for Nathan and Amy in those later years. Their oldest son, Erastus Irwin died in February, 1950 on the farm. Few local records exist of Irwin, as he was called, and what path his life had taken during his 42 years is unclear. A brief genealogical search does show him possibly living in New York for a time in the 1930's and whether or not he lived there permanently is unclear or even whether or not he ever married. Might this have had a hand in the decisions and temperament of Nathan in those later years?

Just as decisions were being made to move forward on the Munger Barn project in the winter and spring of 2000 a serious blow came to the future plans for the farm. The Back to the Future education program came to an abrupt end much to the shock and regret of Tom, me, and the entire Dudley Farm board. Tom and I received a letter from the Connecticut Department of Education informing us that due to the necessity of making cuts to the State education budget most of the programs under the fund we were operating under would be eliminated. As part of an urban/suburban diversity initiative, the funding for Back to the Future had brought over 4000 urban and suburban students to the farm to learn together about 19th century farm life that current school year alone. Not only had Tom and I been able to build a bridge to our shared past for the young students who had come to the farm, we had also been able to help bridge cultural differences that were increasingly separating urban and suburban children in Connecticut.

Our first reaction was to appeal to the state and though the bureaucrats in charge were sympathetic to our plight, they were overwhelmed by like appeals and the bottom line was the money just was not there. We next turned to our local Board of Education through the principle of the High School and the superintendent for the school district to see what we could salvage of the program. Perhaps a scaled back version? Maybe a renewal of the high school class that had made such a difference to the students and farm during those early years? Unfortunately our appeals there fell before the constraints of an ever tightening school budget funded by local property taxes. Barbara Truex, who had been so instrumental in starting the class while the high school principal, now as superintendent could not justify funding Tom and me at the farm for even one class of high school students. Reality was, with a tight budget we could both be brought back to teach classes in our departments and thus eliminate the need to fund a teacher for the equivalent of two classes for each of us. Local and state austerity trumped the value associated with the farm as an educational resource. We were all devastated.

Sadly it became clear that even a community like Guilford that prided itself on its heritage could not and would not continue to fund a unique and successful program at the Dudley Farm for regional students or just those from the community. Short term political and financial considerations had preempted the lasting impact an educational program utilizing the Dudley Farm might have for thousands of children. Tom and I knew that the opportunities to learn at the farm had changed the lives of many of the high school students from Guilford who had participated, and we knew through feedback and evaluations from teachers who had brought their classes, whether first grade or high school, that the programs offered at the farm had been extremely effective as well. But without a commitment from the state or Guilford Public Schools it was over. In vain, we discussed with the board of directors options the Dudley Farm might have to preserve its role in allowing young people the opportunity to learn and in the end none were viable. The cost would be more than the Foundation could afford.

Looking back now, it is quite obvious how important the contributions those Dudley Farm classes from Guilford High were towards the creation of the Dudley Farm as a museum. Tom and I had asked the students to do things beyond the scope of expectations inherent to a typical public school today and they had responded magnificently, and in the process helped save the farm. Through their hands-on labor and learning, through their research and academic efforts, the students of those classes brought a farm and museum to life. There was never a day when Tom and I did not appreciate the opportunity we enjoyed and for both of us seasoned, veteran teachers, we knew this was what true teaching and learning was all about. For that, we will both forever be thankful to the Dudley Foundation for giving us that opportunity. For the thousands of local and statewide students who came to the farm through the *Back to the Future* program, we always knew from their faces how important the visits to the farm were and how they were able, through the various hands on lessons focusing on daily farm chores, seasonal activities, or the experience of 19th century life, to gain a meaningful connection with the past.

It was all quite a blow for the Dudley Foundation. They had come to count on the energy and enthusiasm the children brought to the farm and their presence had given meaning to life and affirmed all the struggles that had brought the farm into existence. As one of the office volunteers said of the children who came on a weekly basis, "one reason why I come here is to see their smiles and hear their laughter". But it was deeper than that. One of the integral parts of the Dudley Foundation mission was to become an educational center, one that would allow the general public and more importantly, their children to gain an appreciation for our heritage as embodied in the farm. Suddenly, one of the cornerstones of that mission was gone and to a certain extent, a sense of betrayal had come home to roost. Those old feelings of "us" versus "them", Cohabit versus Guilford, resurfaced. A sense that the Foundation had reached out to the greater community and been rebuffed began to fester like an old wound. I had to agree. The handle of faith that the Foundation had come to embrace the future with had been sorely tested.

Interlude Number Eleven

(The following testimonials from teachers throughout Connecticut were given to Tom and I about the Back to the Future *program and they had graciously allowed us to reprint them in the brochure we sent out to schools describing the program offerings).*

We believe for most of our students, this will be a lasting experience
—Kindergarten Teacher, New Haven

The kids loved the hands-on activities. They were all involved and that held their interest. We can't wait to come back!
—Grade One Teacher, Guilford

It was an excellent hands-on program for all ages. The staff was exceptional. They were knowledgeable, patient, and full of historical facts! We loved the hands-on activities and farm land.
—Third Grade Teacher, North Branford

Thank you for a very educational and interesting day. The instructors were able to key into our age level and type of students we have.
—Middle School Teacher, Hartford

My class and I thoroughly enjoyed this field trip. It was very informative judging by the wealth of information remembered by my class the next day.
—Fifth Grade Teacher, Meriden

The animals were great – as was the organization of groups and rotating activities! Thanks for a great day!
—Second Grade Teacher, East Haven

I was worried that my students wouldn't be able to understand concepts or complete activities due to the fact that we would be with our buddies (from another district). I was pleased that my students fully participated and were actively engaged in all that the Dudley Farm and its great teachers had to offer. We can't wait to go back again!

— First Grade Teacher, Meriden

The day was fantastic. As always, excellent preparation went into the activities.

—Third Grade Teacher, Guilford

I thought the program was wonderful. The children really enjoyed visiting the Dudley Farm. We look forward to coming back next year.

—Kindergarten Teacher, New Haven[8]

Chapter Twelve

Raising the Dream

*The future belongs to those
who believe in the beauty of their dreams.*
—Eleanor Roosevelt

The fall of 2000 had a different feel than those of the recent past at the farm. Without the presence of school children, the farm seemed to fall into a sort of a daily slumber. The volunteers at the office still came every day for their three hour shifts, giving tours when visitors and the curious stopped by, sending out mailings, and answering the phone. The Saturday farmers market was in full gear until the end of October and was busier than ever while hundreds attended our annual Farm Day. But the overall atmosphere had changed, as when a family gathering for a holiday is first held following the death of a loved one. To compound the feeling of malaise, Kristie had moved on from the farm leaving us without a director of events and by then the Friday Night series had run its course. Like the farm of the Dudley's in 1900, ours had taken on an air of permanence mixed with a drowsy loss of purpose. It was confusing and frustrating for many of us on the board and though we knew things had changed, we were still determined to make the best of the situation and move forward. We turned our energy to the Munger Barn and what it would mean to the farm's future. We still believed in our dream.

It was a strange and in many ways surreal time for me as curator at the farm the winter and spring of 2001. Once again teaching at the high school full time, I stopped by the farm three days or so after work each week to catalogue donated items that had become part of the farm's growing collection since the early 1990's, return phone calls, and deal with the farms correspondence. My goal was to continue to organize and build the Dudley Farm into a museum that would reflect the standards held by more established historic institutions. With no real budget and with no realistic possibility of having one, I did the best I could with the help of others when they could. I catalogued, set up the rooms in the house, cleaned up the barns where possible, and put together displays in the limited space available in the house. I found the work satisfying in that I knew that every bit I did helped make the museum become more of a reality, but often felt frustrated that what I could do was so limited. I presented new plans to the board to reorganize how the farm operated; hoping to create committees once again that might develop programs, proposals for improvements, and accomplish work that could continue the mission of the Foundation. But without the desire or ability of members to move forward on them, I began to feel like a swimmer treading water.

I often found solace in the farm itself and on those many afternoons as I went about my business I felt reassured by the nature of the place and a sense that though frustrated by setbacks, on a whole, we had brought life back to the farm and we might still bring life to the dreams we had for its future. There were times, when I walked through the house, strolled the grounds, or rummaged about the barns that I felt I was not alone, that the spirit of one or more Dudley was with me, watching in a curious and supportive manner. By then I was convinced that the very essence of what people felt at the farm certainly had something to do with its rustic charm and beauty, but that there was more, a spiritual quality that visitors often mentioned they felt. Sure it was a charming old New England house and farm, and its very nature had a feel that was much different than most homes and dwellings in our more modern environment. Yet there was a presence somehow, a calming and reassuring one that we all felt in our own way which helped us to find the fortitude and desire to continue. Each of us had developed our own sense of mission by it and through it.

I often think back to a day when the farm saw roughly 60 young students visit through the Back to the Future program. They were young kids, maybe second or third grade, some from Guilford and others from New Haven, and they had been paired together for a series of activities in which they could experience 19th century life. As always, the children were a delight to work with and responded well to every task, question, and activity as they gained a better understanding of the past as well as each other. But as is sometimes the case, a parent who had volunteered to chaperone might have been better off staying home. Because we usually broke the students into small groups of eight to ten with a chaperone or two to go through various activity stations, we usually had one to four independent study high school students working with us manning the stations along with Tom and me.

One of our high school helpers accompanied a group into the house just as I was exiting with another quietly let me know that one mother was causing a stressful situation, complaining about every aspect of the visit, and making both her and the students increasingly uncomfortable. I asked if she would like to exchange groups and she quickly agreed. We switched and I began the tour of the house with her former group, walking the kids through each room, describing each and its contents, answering questions and describing how life was different in a 1900 house than today. Every step of the way, the chaperone eagerly volunteered a negative comment, about each room, how it was set up, or why conditions were dangerous for the children, thus casting a negative spell as we moved from room to room. The students from New Haven gazed at her in nervous amazement while those from Guilford looked sheepishly away. I'm not sure who her son or daughter was, since he or she were certainly lying low. Not amused, I tried to diffuse as many of her comments as I could, politely answering her questions and trying to ignore her statements. By the time we walked down the back staircase from the second floor to the dining room, she was in a full fury, complaining about the danger of the old stairs for children and visitors alike and how we were irresponsible allowing anyone to traverse them.

It was soon after that moment, as we were exiting the dining room and out onto the porch that I knew there was a spirit to the house that was sympathetic to our efforts. Just as she stepped onto the porch and was about to step down onto the grassy lawn she tumbled forward landing on her hands and knees. She sprang up and in a startled voice shouted that she had been pushed or kicked in her behind, a blow that had sent her sprawling. The fact that she had been the last person out the door with no one behind her other than me and I was still in the dining room at the time, vindicated us all though if having been given the chance, who knows? Embarrassed, she repeated her story and at that moment the kids from New Haven burst out in laughter followed by the Guilford kids too. There were no further comments on her behalf for the rest of the visit and though she was clearly uninjured, her pride certainly was.

Later, after the students and their erstwhile chaperone left, I reiterated the event to Tom and the student who had been so afflicted during her visit. Through our laughter, we all agreed that she had either been clumsy and fallen or that a spirit from the house, annoyed by her negativity and critical comments, had given her the boot. Our student agreed without a doubt who had given her an assist—David, and Tom and I had to agree. We always had sensed that a benevolent presence was at home on the farm and in the house in particular, and it seemed to have affirmed our feelings with one good, firm kick. As the other high school students learned of the incident they all joined in and agreed; it had been David.

At the annual meeting that October we decided to announce the plan to move ahead with the Munger Barn project with a very optimistic goal of raising the frame that next July. Once again elected president, it was my pleasure to speak on behalf of the board of directors that despite the setback caused by the end of the education program the Foundation was still looking forward to the future and that future was embodied in the Munger Barn and it's raising. We would hold an old fashioned barn raising during which the timber frame would be assembled and raised by hand, timber by timber just as it had been done for over 300 years. The raising would be a community event with farm members, volunteers, and the community invited to participate and celebrate in a rare historic opportunity. To make it all happen, I announced that through the efforts of State Representatives Bob Ward and Pat Widlitz, who represented North Guilford and Guilford in the State Legislature, as well as that of then Guilford First Selectman Sam Bartlett, the Dudley Farm had received a $25,000 grant from a State fund to enhance historic preservation and tourism. Thanks to their efforts, we now had the seed money needed to raise additional funds for the project. Following those announcements, the featured speaker was North Guilford resident and Foundation member Jonathan Wuerth, well known throughout Connecticut for his skillful work restoring antique homes and barns. Wuerth's topic was old barns and outbuildings and why and how they were worth saving. We left the meeting primed and ready.

At our weekly board meetings that November, it became clear that despite our optimistic forecast of raising the barn by the coming summer, it was obvious that we were far from ready. Despite the design work done by Doug and lots of legwork by Henry and others, we were in no way ready to tackle the project, either financially or logistically. We debated long and hard over how to finance the raising and once again it came down to two camps; pay as we go or finance the project. Locked in the same old dance, the patience of each partner grew thin as toes were stepped on and each attempt at reconciliation recalled the old tired songs of years gone by. We were stuck.

A break in the impasse that had led to our paralysis thankfully came. Mark Dudley, who along with board member Janet and their son Evan were the livestock committee for the farm and cared for the assortment of animals, some theirs, some the farm's, approached me about several conversations with barn builder and restorer George Senerchia he had recently. In the late 1990's, George, his wife Susan, and partner Gene Jones, who were *Northford Timber Framers*, had restored one of the other barns taken from the Munger property into an artist's studio and addition to a house in the neighboring town of Madison. George had occasionally run into Mark while working on that project and eventually Mark broached the idea of getting involved with the Dudley Farm's raising. George expressed a willingness to consider the project and I enthusiastically asked Mark to approach the board with the possibility. Along with a few others on the Board of Directors, I jumped at the opportunity to enlist his help and soon after a number of us visited George at his home workshop in the next door village of Northford, eager to see his work and find out what he had to say. I for one felt this might be our best and possibly only chance at making the dream of the barn a reality for the farm and was immediately convinced that George was our man as we drove up his drive and into a collection of meticulously restored antique 18th and 19th century barns. Henry, Tom, Doug, Mark and I talked for a long time with George about the art of timber framing, his passion for the old way of building, and his love of barns as we toured those he had restored on his property. We were all convinced. But was he? As George eagerly said, he had always been a sucker for an old timber frame and he knew this would be love at first sight though I worried once he got a look at the frame stored in that old container truck, not even a shotgun wedding could make it all happen. But for now all that was left was to convince the rest of the board, let George have a look at the frame, get him and Doug to sit down with the plans, and of course, figure out how to pay for it all.

Despite the hesitation of some board members to invite an outsider to take on the task of restoring, preserving, and retrofitting the Munger Barn frame, a general consensus was reached that George was our man once he attended a board meeting and spoke of his plan for the frame and a raising that would follow. His enthusiasm was contagious and his eagerness to begin working on the frame was infectious. This man loved a timber frame and as he spoke it was clear that his passion went way beyond the pieces that composed the structure. George seemed to channel the very essence of those long ago craftsmen who had first made the frame and that emotional and psychological connection lent to him an aura of confidence and purpose that could only be likened to one whose mission in life was a crusade to save every barn that was left.

By December, George and Gene had retrieved the frame from the rusting trailer and hauled it the eight miles to their shop in Northford. Their first task was to inspect each component of the frame and get a sense of what was usable and what would have to be replaced, then sit down with Doug and Henry to review the plans drawn up for the barn's new life. Together they worked out the seemingly thousands of details involved in not only preserving and resurrecting a 100 year old building, but retrofitting it to meet the needs of the Foundation and modern building codes. By that winter, it was still hoped that a community raising might take place that summer but as March turned to April the possibility seemed more and more remote. The magnitude of the work, not just on the frame, but on the site itself came home to roost. New timbers needed to be found, shaped, and integrated with the old into the structure as the design of the frame itself continuously evolved to meet growing list of modern safety requirements dictated by the barn's use as a public space for events and activities. Permits had to be filed, accepted, and issued by the town before the site work could begin, the old stone foundation where the 18th century barn had stood removed, and a new concrete one put in its place. The framing of the deck, window and door placement, heating, plumbing, electricity, and all the other hundreds of elements so vital to the building had to be worked out and included in the mix. Volunteer labor had to be secured and donations of materials solicited when possible; in this Henry and Bob Ashman worked a continual round of miracles. And then there was the financing.

Financing of the project was slow and tedious, with many members of the board and the Foundation helping to raise the funds needed to pay the expanding pile of bills related to the project. Not only did *Northford Timber Framers* have to be paid, materials not donated had to be paid for as well. In a wonderful historic connection, George was able to find replacement timbers for many of the frame parts that were either too far gone, needed replacing to meet building codes, or were dictated by design changes at a saw mill in Guilford, Vermont, located just north of the Massachusetts border. Guilford, Vermont had been settled just before the American Revolution by residents of Guilford, Connecticut as part of a general migration north into what would later become the Green Mountain State. Thousands had moved northward in search of land during the years following the final English victory over the French in Canada in 1763 that had opened the region to settlement by land hungry citizens from Connecticut towns and many from Guilford and North Guilford were among those swarming northward up the Connecticut River. For many of us working hard to see the Munger Barn raised, the symbolic connection of the home of the timbers only added to our sense of purpose in pursuing the goal of bringing history to life through its raising.

Through the efforts of many board members, among them Janet Dudley, Linda Curry, and Doug Williamson, loans to complete the anticipated funding of the project were secured from *The Guilford Savings Bank* and *The Guilford Preservation Alliance*. Ultimately, the loans, combined with the state grant, donations from Foundation and community members, and Dudley Foundation savings, made it all come together.

But in May, just as it seemed we might be ready for that July, the unexpected happened and the planned raising had to be postponed. Reality struck in two ways; fund raising had run into a few delays and would not be completed by the summer and a looming personal crisis had developed for George. He would need a heart transplant.

It was stunningly shocking that the person whose energy and determination was driving the Munger project forward after years of stagnation was suddenly facing a daily life and death situation. George and his enthusiasm had reinvigorated our vision for the farm but now that did not matter. As the pace of his work slowed, we assured him that we could carry on without him and that the frame was of no consequence compared to his health. We each assumed that George would, out of necessity, end his involvement in order to concentrate on his medical condition and lamented the shear personal tragedy this all meant for him and his family. But with George, we had already learned to expect the unexpected; he not only wanted to continue working on the frame, he wanted to finish the project and supervise its raising. Along with the others on the board, I worried about having him continue until I saw how working on the frame affected him, encouraged him to reconsider. George passionately explained that retrofitting and preserving the frame was an important part of who he was and that having it to work on would not only help him deal with his condition, it would help him work his way through it. Before his determined appeal we had to relent. Amazingly in the end, the efforts of George and Gene in resurrecting the frame would far outpace the rest of our efforts.

It turned out, the delays proved an unanticipated blessing as we were able to regroup and refocus our efforts in regard to every aspect of the project. At the time however, many of us felt frustrated by what became an increasingly emotional tangle of issues that at times seemed to make the barn raising more and more improbable. One thing I had learned about the Dudley Foundation board of directors over the years was that time was sometimes not necessarily a good thing when it came to any project or plan undertaken. I do not believe a harder working, more dedicated group of individuals could be found anywhere once a project was initiated, which was one of the organization's true strengths. But when there were delays or time to second guess decisions that had been collectively made, dissension and dispute often followed. This was simply a part of the group's decision making dynamic. As summer turned to autumn that year, often contentious disagreements began to surface over just about every aspect of the project; from how the barn would be used to the work in progress or that still needed to be done. My role as president was taking on more of a referee flavor than I cared for at a time when it was becoming increasingly evident that I needed to devote more time to my role as curator due to the blossoming growth of that aspect of the museum. It seemed a good time for a change and I decided to step down in October when a new president could be selected at the annual meeting.

Graciously Janet Dudley stepped forward to take over that fall and was unanimously elected by those farm members attending the annual meeting. Since joining the Foundation in the mid 1990's, Janet had become an important contributor to the development of the farm as a museum in every aspect of its operation, from bringing animals to the farm, taking charge of the Heritage Garden, or donating her time and considerable historical knowledge and skills to just about every event and effort. When Kristie Rubendunst had moved on from her position as event co-coordinator, Janet had taken on the responsibility as a member of the board. She also brought with her valuable contacts with the downtown historic community where she had been involved for years and those contacts helped to integrate the Dudley Farm more fully with those organizations. Most importantly, her calm and pleasant demeanor lent itself immediately to every discussion and issue. In essence, Janet was exactly what the Dudley Foundation needed at that moment. I stayed on as vice president to assist her in navigating the pitfalls and nuances associated with leadership of a nonprofit in general and specifically the Dudley Foundation, having dealt with the politics inherent to the organization for so many years.

As the spring of 2002 began, we all realized that it was, in fact, going to be possible to raise the Munger Barn frame that coming summer as George and Gene continued their reworking of its many parts and plans were finalized for the site work, foundation, decking, and design. Windows and doors were ordered and siding decided on, and plans began for a community barn raising, the likes of which Guilford and the region had not seen for well over 100 years. Excitement grew in anticipation and the board chose the weekend of August 24th for what promised to be a tremendous triumph of sorts for the Foundation. After six years of working towards the goal of raising the Munger Barn on the footprint of the old Dudley one, it was all coming together as that April Henry led the charge to prepare the site and pour the foundation walls. The Munger Barn represented the start of a new era for the Dudley Farm, and as that spring turned to June, then July, last minute details were attended to as the deck went on and as a group we all recognized that with each step in the process we were securing the farm for future generations.

As Henry and Bob worked tirelessly, and volunteers helped as they could, the pace quickened. While George and Gene wrapped up their work on the frame others moved full throttle into the planning of the community raising. Word went out to save the date and I devoted most of the June 2002 *Farm News* newsletter to the anticipated event. In one of the articles devoted to the barn raising, I described how:

> …important they were to the life of a community such as Guilford for centuries. It was a job beyond the ability of a few men to accomplish and it gave neighbors and friends a chance to work together to build more than a barn; they built and renewed their sense of common purpose and community. Their efforts brought about a common bond that gave them a connection to who they were and a sense that they were all part of a greater good.[1]

At the barn raising, our plan was to rekindle that sense of community and common purpose that had been so integral to the creation of the Dudley Farm ten years before following David Dudley's gifting of the farm to the fire company. In hosting an old fashioned raising and celebration, we asked both Dudley Farm members and friends to attend on Saturday and Sunday to help out as they could or just watch and help celebrate the event. The general public was invited as well. The celebration would be a thank you to the community for ten years of support and showcase the farm and the progress we had made. Work would begin each day at 8:00 am and a traditional barn raising celebration with food and music would take place late Sunday afternoon once the frame was up. For all involved, it would be a once in a lifetime opportunity.

Also in the June edition of the *Farm News*, I had asked George if he felt up to contributing an article describing the restoration process of the barn frame. In his usual enthusiastic fashion, he agreed and submitted the following; *The Story of a Late 19th Century Barn*:

The Munger Barn started its life with an agricultural purpose. Most 19th century Connecticut hay barns were 40ft in length with four bents. This would give a 12ft center bay and two 14 foot bays on either side. Our barn is very similar to this except it has two 18 foot side bays and an oversized center bay. The two large hay lofts would have stored a great amount of hay over the winter. Eventually our barn became part of the Munger Lumber Company which existed in Madison into the 1990's. There were several barns that were dismantled from the Munger property. Little did I know that we [Northford Timber Framers], would restore or maybe resurrect would be a better word, the two largest.

The first one we restored was made into an artist's studio and a handsome addition onto a house in Madison. In 2000, I was contacted by the Dudley Foundation to see if we could save and re-erect the larger of the two Munger barns. The first time I met our 1890 frame it had been stored in a container truck at the Dudley Farm for a number of years. We brought the entire timber frame to my shop in Northford where we began the long process of cataloging each timber and making drawings of each member.

We were able to get a hands-on look at a late 19th century timber frame and get a sense of how the framing techniques had changed over 300 years of timber framing. By 1890, the Victorian Era was in full swing and a transition period in the building techniques of homes and barns was taking place. Timber framing was in its decline and the highly skilled craftsmen of the earlier part of the 19th century who still had a connection to "roots" barns were gone. The process of timber framing had begun to be watered down and kind of cheapened if you will. Balloon framing was on the rise and stick framing was the future.

This being said, it made the process of sorting out good timbers from unusable very difficult because being skilled timber framers, we can reproduce new sound timbers very easily but the character that an old barn has and the warmth and glow of antique wood cannot be duplicated. We thus had to use our skills to marry old timbers with new ones to replace those that were rotten; the result was a tremendous combination of the past and the future.

We designed the two large bays to accommodate second floor loft areas. Our barn will make a beautiful learning center, farmer's market, museum, great place to hang out, and terrific addition to the Dudley Farm. We are also proud to have been given the opportunity to save this humble building and turn it into something special and one of a kind for the Dudley Farm Museum. To save the past farm architecture of our country and state is very satisfying and rewarding. If we lose the past, we'll all have nothing. So saving this barn is an accomplishment that the entire group of volunteers at the Dudley Farm deserve our congratulations and thanks. The people of Guilford and all of Connecticut are proud of you all!

On August 24th and 25th we will be having our barn raising at the Dudley Farm and a chance to give back to the landscape a piece of America's past—a barn. To me time will stand still. I wish I could bring the entire world to see that we can and will always come together as friends and neighbors to help each other, to help our community, and to help our country.

So please everyone, come out and support us as we raise the past into the future at the Dudley Farm. We are asking the community of Guilford and all the friends of the Dudley Farm to support our efforts to rebuild this barn. Approximately 200 white oak pegs or treenails will be needed for the frame to be raised. They have recently been made and we are asking everyone to stop by the Dudley Farm and purchase one which will be autographed individually or as a family for a donation. The pegs will then be used to secure the mortise and tenon joinery in the frame. So come on Guilford, show your stuff and become one of the builders of the barn.

Barns have texture and character that connect us to the earliest Americans; settlers and patriots. Most importantly, barns have souls. The Munger Barn will begin its new life with our soul. Please support us, come on out, and help out.[2]

One of the remarkable things about an old timber frame for a person of our time is the fact that they were constructed like a giant puzzle, each individual part dependent on others and meticulously fit together using gravity and a system called mortise and tenons. A mortise is a pocket cut out of a timber and a tenon was the tapered and shaped end of another timber that fit snuggly into the mortise. Once fit together, their weight and gravity would lock them in place. But to secure the timbers and prevent their separating, a special wooden device was used; a trunnel. So what's a trunnel? In the June 2002 *Farm News* I described them:

Timber frame buildings like the Munger Barn have been around for a very long time. In Europe, there are still many standing that were built during the Middle Ages and the building technique may actually date back to the time of the ancient Romans. That's a pretty good pedigree.

In Connecticut, there are thousands of houses and barns that date back to the 18th and early 19th centuries. Guilford alone has one of the largest inventories of 18th century houses (and older) in the country. What has allowed these homes to stand so long as functioning symbols of the past? The timber frame by which they were built. Their massive post and beam timbers fit together with mortise and tenon joints have stood the test of time. But there is more to their secret of longevity. There is the trunnel.

Early American builders as well as their English and Medieval ancestors knew that to use iron nails to fasten wooden timbers together would doom the frame to eventual death. Why? Because over time the oxidation of metal (rust) would create rot in the wood around it. Eventually the rot would become so extensive the frame would weaken and the structure might collapse. This, combined with the high cost of iron made the use of nails prohibitive. The solution—trunnels.

So what is a trunnel? As you may have already guessed or know, it's a treenail. The word itself is old English, literally a wooden nail. During the 17th through 19th centuries, trunnels were used extensively in timber framing and in ship building in Connecticut. For many farmers, making trunnels was a good rainy day or winter activity that brought a little extra when sold or traded. Trunnels were always in demand. Today we know trunnels by their more common and less romantic name—pegs.[3]

In order to keep the mortise and tenon joint secure, a hole was drilled through the side of the timber that held the mortise, through the tenon , and out the other side of the mortised timber. This hole, roughly one inch in diameter, would then have the trunnel hammered into it, tightening the joint and keeping it from coming apart or twisting as the timbers dried and shrank or expanded in humidity depending on the weather. The trunnel itself was shaped from a piece of oak and was about an inch or more longer than the width of the mortised timber that had been rounded with a tool called a shaving knife in order to fit tightly into the hole. The result was the joining together of two pieces of the timber frame that were now close to impossible to separate and incredibly strong. This was how the Munger Barn frame was to be put together.

The article about trunnels continued:

When the Munger Barn frame is raised this August it will need more than 200 trunnels. Shaped from pieces of oak, they will literally hold the frame together and allow the barn to stand. As you have already read, George and the Dudley Farm's friends at Northford Timber Framers have made them and you now have the opportunity to purchase a trunnel that will go into the frame for $25. Symbolic of our working together to raise the barn, each trunnel is individually numbered and will be signed by the person making the donation. Just think, your name or that of a loved one as a lasting memorial to the resurrection of the Munger Barn and its new life. By purchasing a trunnel, you will help fund the restoration and the raising of that old timber frame, and help hold it together for another century or more—sort of like a trunnel.[4]

The response to this fund raiser was overwhelming. But more important, it introduced the greater community to the purpose behind the raising, to bring us all together in a way seldom experienced in our modern lives. The simple act of buying a trunnel, volunteering to help with the raising of the frame, helping with the celebration during and afterwards, or just being there to watch and support the effort cut to the very essence of why the Dudley Farm existed and awoke in us all a spiritual connection to those who had lived before us. It was an affirmation of who we were or maybe hoped to be. It was the simple beauty of our dream becoming reality.

Interlude Number Twelve

(I found this poem on the internet by a poet named Sam Jackson. It beautifully describes the life of an old barn and the unfortunate fate of many, but not the Munger Barn thanks to all who contributed to its rebirth on the Dudley Farm).

Old Barns And Men

Its Boards are loose, and warped, and weathered.
  Shingles flyin' in the wind.
Timbers leanin', ridge pole sags.
  A hundred seasons done it in.

Settin' lonesome, sad, neglected,
  seems to sense it's end is near.
Recollections long forgot—of
  friends with hammers workin' here.

Status once was never questioned,
  vital structure in its day.
Uses that this shelter rendered—
  far beyond just 'storin' hay'.

Stood majestic, stately, noble.
  Stout design, yet gentle charm.
Served as banner to the world;
  message was: "Successful Farm!"

Answered all whose glance might query
  lineage of the builders clan
who tilled surrounding fertile fields
  to earn their living off this land.

Proudly served each generation,
  guarding them in work and play,
thirsting not for acclamation,
  'care' was more than ample pay.

Hidden back in every shadow,
  clues and scars of past events;
'Jackson fork', it's tines a rustin',
  lies beneath the fallen fence.

Inside, hangs the fraying fibers,
  once a hay rope dangled there.
Listen closely, hear the laughter?
  Children swingin' through the air.

Climb the loft, there in a corner,
  boards once blackened by a fire.
Boys a smokin' pipes of corn silk,
  dealt with sternly by their sire!

Reckon sounds of men at work as
  tons of hay are hoisted in.
Ropes'er creakin', pulleys squeakin',
  horses neigh above the din.

Soon winters cloak of frozen whiteness
  covers fields and pasture land.
The barns importance more apparent,
  inside doors now seems more grand.

Amply storing food and fiber,
  walls to break the winters gale,
"haven" seems well to describe'er,
  guests within stay hearty, hale.

Time moves on and progress quickens,
  new techniques come into play.
Less reliant on the farmstead,
  children grow, then move away.

Oldsters now are those remaining,
  seeing things once only dreams;
tractor chuggin' up the furrows
  now out works a dozen teams.

With time required for its nurture
  crowded out by other chores,
the barns demise is now beginning—
  'modern times' the predators.

This reminisce makes quite apparent;
  'Old Barns and men, are much the same',
When young and useful—both have value—
  When old, the world, forgets their name!

Chapter Thirteen

Raising Redemption

Seeking to forget makes exile all the longer;
the secret of redemption lies in remembrance.
— RICHARD VON WEIZSAECKER

L ooking back it is clear that the experience of the barn raising was the culmination of ten remarkable years of trying to create not just the Dudley Farm as a museum, but to rekindle a sense of community whose loss had been integral to the saving of the farm to begin with. Little did we know, as von Weizsaecker said, how our increasing cultural exile from the past had led us all, through the experience of saving the farm, to a redemption of sorts. What had started as an effort to save a symbol of a quickly vanishing world had become a crusade to preserve, recreate, and perpetuate what once was so common for not only us, but future generations; a remembrance of what once was. In that struggle, we each found our own personal reconciliation with the past, not as an abstract myth or idea, but as a tangible reality. As we worked to reawaken that same sense in the community that had formed around the farm, we hoped to share with them an understanding of what that past truly was. The symbol and vehicle of that redemption was the Munger Barn

Raising the frame would be a dramatic and romantic moment, but prior to that, a tremendous amount of labor had to go into preparing the mountain of timbers once they arrived on the site prior to assembling them into sections called bents. It was here that George was at his best. Three days before the raising, the timbers, both old and new, were brought to the area just outside the fully decked foundation for their final organizing and processing. A good number of the newer timbers had to have their mortises and tenons cut, brought together with their fellow pieces to form a section, and then moved to the floor of the barn. Like a general directing his troops into battle, George organized those of us there to shape, cut, and create the joints, move each timber into position, and ready each part for the raising Saturday morning. For three days we hauled, cut, shaved, and coated each timber with an organic preservative in preparation for the big day. Through it all, George unflaggingly seemed to be everywhere; on the deck, directing the placement of a mortise, explaining why a particular timber was shaped as it was, or simply shouting encouragement. Here was a man whose heart was functioning at less than 20% seemingly everywhere in the hot, humid sun of August, cheering us on and cajoling us in his good natured way; a human dynamo of activity. It was truly remarkable. He seemed to literally be channeling the very spirits of those long ago craftsmen for whom what we were doing was so routine, and as the sun grew stronger each day, so it seemed, did George.

The process of raising a timber frame by hand, especially one as large as that of the Munger Barn, was a logistical feat that required organization, muscle power, and teamwork; a rarity in our modern, machine driven era. For the Dudley's, a raising would have taken place in much the same way we were planning it and I for one, felt confident that we were going to experience something magically historic. Yet as we each arrived at the farm early that summer morning, you could feel the excitement wrapped in apprehension as thick as the moist, humid air. Whereas the Dudley's, even as late as 1900, would have been familiar with the process, the work, and communal environment in which a raising would take place, for most of us it was a new and a bit intimidating experience. The number of timbers that made up the frame, their placement, the amount of labor required, and the magnitude of the job seemed dauntingly impossible to accomplish in a weekend. Were we, the now 21st century heirs to the Dudley's and their neighbors up to the task?

For one thing, the number of people needed to raise the frame was significant, on average an estimated one person was required for every 50 pounds of weight to be lifted. We knew in advance that a good number of Foundation members and volunteers from the community were planning to participate, but how many could actually help raise the frame and for how long might they be able to help was the question. Then there was the actual celebration that would take place during the raising both days; were we ready for the number of spectators that might stop by, could we accommodate them all and keep everyone safe while keeping the atmosphere casual, comfortable, and historic? We quickly found out as the lower field used for parking filled to overflowing. This we all agreed was going to be something.

Perhaps it might be best to briefly explain exactly how a timber frame is raised. The typical timber frame, like the Munger Barn, has four sections called bents. Each bent consists of four posts, two corner posts on each end and two others each one third of the way across. Each bent, three stories high, when raised would span across the lesser width of the 50^{ft} x 30^{ft} foot barn, the width of the gable end. Besides the posts, each bent also included three crossing girts that spanned the distance from corner post to corner post, one half way up the posts, a second another story up, and a third across the top. The girts were locked into the posts with a mortise, tenon, and trunnel and with diagonal braces called knee braces to keep them joined at a 90 degree angle. Prior to the raising, each bent had to be put together on the deck and piled one on another in the reverse order in which they would be raised with the last bent on the bottom and the first one on the top. They were positioned where the last bent was to be located so as each in sequence could be lifted into place. Just off the deck, all the connecting frame pieces were stacked also in sequence of use with the later ones on the bottom and the earlier ones towards the top. These included the girts that would connect the bents, corner braces, second floor joists, and rafters.

Once the raising was to begin, those assembled to raise the frame would stand inside the stacked bents in preparation for lifting the first into position. On command, everyone would lift together until the top girt of the bent was about breast high. Others would then join in and shoulder the posts to aid in the lifting. The trick here was to lift with the legs and not the back as George would incessantly remind us. At that moment the pike men would join in as well. They held long 30 foot poles with sharpened ends called pikes which they pushed against the top girt and upper portions of the posts. Their job was to steady the frame as it rose and as the frame became upright, were joined by pike men on the other side who helped hold the frame and keep it from tumbling forward. At this point, the most delicate maneuver in raising a bent happened. While being held upright, it needed to be walked and persuaded to drop into mortises cut into the sills through the deck of the barn. Each post had a tenon fashioned at its end and the trick was to slide them into place without damaging them or losing the bent by allowing it to slip and fall forward or back, possibly injuring those holding it. To help prevent the posts from sliding, large stop blocks were secured to the deck next to the mortises and in theory the post would simply fall into place.

As each bent slipped into position it was temporarily secured with two braces that ran at an angle from each corner post to the sill. Then as each subsequent bent was raised, the six connecting girts were positioned between them to solidly join the two bents together, one midway up each post and the other across the top. These girts along with knee braces between each girt and post were then secured with trunnels, locking the entire frame. So there it was; it all seemed so easy as we all gathered around the timbers that Saturday awaiting orders from George and anticipating the moment. With a lot of heavy lifting and teamwork, we hoped to see it all come together as a gratifying example of life from a past that until now had only existed in our imaginations. Then we'd celebrate together our triumphant resurrection of the barn and the new life it would have on the farm.

As we chatted anxiously and those of us on the board dealt with those last minute details that accompany any event, the cars and trucks kept coming. By 8:00 am there was no room left to park and cars were being moved up to the upper meadow to accommodate the growing crowd of volunteers and spectators. Our call to help, witness, and celebrate the raising had touched people from the community and beyond. While volunteers streamed towards the deck and a growing crowd gathered around it, George and Janet did their best to bring order to the moment as we all began to feel ourselves entering a portal of sorts into another time.

What happened next was an unforgettable experience for all who came to help or watch; a chance to not just connect with the past, but to experience it and in so doing create for each of us our own sense of purpose and reconciliation with it. At that moment, on a small farm in a rapidly changing community, the ghosts of those who once were stood shoulder to shoulder with us. We knew because we could feel their presence as we lifted the frame, sat on the hill watching, or served a bottle of water to a thirsty volunteer or visitor. It wasn't just our day, it was theirs as well. The comfort of their presence motivated us all as we felt the warm thanks of their remembrance. Or was it the warming sunlight playing on our imaginations?

In the Dudley Farm Newsletter, *Farm News*, Fall 2002, I wrote about the raising as I saw and felt it, and captured what for many of us was the experience:

> ... It was an experience beyond expectations, a chance to see, live, and make history. Volunteers and spectators came from down the road and across Connecticut; from Guilford and North Guilford, Clinton, Madison, New Haven, and Durham. They came from Northford, Middletown, Hamden, Manchester, Stafford, and New Milford. Each for their own reasons; some for curiosity, some out of conviction, or simply avocation. For all it was for the experience, the anticipation of being part of something here to fore only found within their imaginations.
>
> Some came to work or contribute in any way they could. Others to watch, knowing that what they would see would be truly special. For two days they gathered knowing they were part of something wonderful and unique, a piece of history, a glimpse of the past. They arrived as individuals and left as a community, they lived history, they raised a barn. It is easy to dismiss what happened as a fanciful attempt to recreate the past, that what happened was an excuse to play out the dream of what the experience of a community barn raising was all about. But from the very moment volunteers and spectators gathered on and around the deck where the bents lay stacked, waiting to rise, it was obvious something different was happening. There was a reverent excitement and anticipation that struck us all. It was spiritual, almost church-like, as if our 19th

century ancestors were reaching through time, to clasp our hands in eager willingness to help and guide us in our efforts.

As Janet stood to speak the crowd hushed itself quickly. As Foundation president, she welcomed both volunteers and spectators to what she believed to be not just a new beginning for the Munger Barn, but for the Dudley Farm as well. She thanked all those who had volunteered long hours to get us to that moment and those individuals and businesses that had helped through generous gifts and donations. Janet then introduced the Reverend John Van Epps of the North Guilford Congregational Church whose blessing not only inspired us but connected this day to that time before the Dudley Farm was even an idea and the Fire Company and his church had first received David's generous gift. For those of us who had worked so hard over the past ten years to bring the farm to life, his blessing was a special spiritual validation of that struggle. The Rev. Van Epps was followed by First Selectman Carl Balestracci whose comments commended the role the Dudley Farm has played in not only preserving a vital part of local history but also for its mission to share that past with the public. Then State Senator Bill Aniskovich, who had been instrumental in helping to create the Dudley Foundation, presented to Janet a framed *Resolution of Appreciation and Congratulation* from the Connecticut General Assembly to the Dudley Farm for its efforts in building a community through continued efforts to preserve the past.

With that, the raising began. All eyes turned to George as he slowly climbed onto the stack of timbers waiting to be raised. He spoke of timber framing and its connection to those who had come before us and the importance of being aware of that past as we worked to resurrect the Munger frame so it could begin its new life as part of the Dudley Farm. The gathering community, led by the 30 or so volunteers on the deck, all eager to begin their work, focused on every word, drinking in his passion and enthusiasm for what was about to take place. George then described what we were about to experience, the steps involved, the importance of safety, and his hope that we all would find for ourselves a meaning in what was about to happen.

As the first bent was readied and George reiterated how we needed to work as one, be focused on his commands, and that there was no turning back or stopping once the lift began, the silence felt eerie in its heaviness. Then it happened, the moment when time stood still and the past merged with the present. Energized by the spirits of his long gone fellow craftsmen, George began the spell, his voice loud and clear despite his health; "lift, lift, lift!" At that instant he embodied the very essence of the moment through his presence as eager shoulders, arms, and legs strained to lift the timbers of the bent off the deck. The shadow of history engulfed the farm and transformed us all through time and space. We were living the past and it was magic.

Straining to the weight we lifted, the only sound to be heard was George's bellowing voice, directing and encouraging us. "Lift, lift" he exhorted. Then suddenly the call "Pike poles! Pike poles!" and the long sticks appeared seemingly out of nowhere steadying the bent as it lurched to an upright position. But the frame was not yet in place, balancing a good two feet or so from its four mortises positioned along the gable end facing the Durham Road. On George's command, the bent rose as if levitating above the deck by the shear will of those lifting and balanced by the pike men, it floated across those precarious inches to its waiting mortises. "Jonathan!" yelled George and as if by magic, Jonathan Wuerth appeared armed with an enormous wooden mallet called a commander, who slammed the base of each post helping each slide into its home. With all posts secured, the silence was dramatically broken by the spontaneous cheers and applause of those watching from the hill just above the site joined quickly by the workers still clinging to the posts and pike poles on the deck. Until temporary braces were attached to hold it in place, none dared move.

Quickly the braces went up and those who had raised the frame broke into an elated orgy of hugs, back slapping, handshakes and cheers as we congratulated ourselves, blending our voices with the roar of those watching. We had done it; we had raised that first bent. And though one bent, does not make a barn, we reveled in our accomplishment and the camaraderie of the moment. There it was, standing in the bright August sun, the first of four; the Munger Barn had begun its new life. This small piece of history had been saved, preserved for the future. But for those of us there, something had changed. We had returned from our exile, we were renewed through the meaning of our efforts; like those posts, we were home.

For the rest of the day and all of the next, work continued as the other three bents were raised then connected together with girts and braces. Hundreds came to watch history reborn, some for just a while, others for the hours on end. Throughout the day equally hard working volunteers served food donated by local individuals and businesses, making sure all involved got more than enough to eat. Through it all, the indomitable *Dudley Farm String Band*, formed out of those monthly Saturday jams back in the 1990's, played on, entertaining and encouraging workers and spectators alike with a mix of old time folk and blue grass music. At noon, work was halted so that all could witness and take part in a Native American blessing ceremony conducted by long time Dudley Foundation member Gordon "Fox Running" Brainerd. In a solemn prayer, he asked that the structure and all who were there be blessed as well as all who would enter the barn in the future. Later, once the barn had been completed, Fox Running would create a small yet poignant museum highlighting the culture of the areas original Algonquian inhabitants from his extensive personal collection of artifacts. Located in the second floor loft area of the barn, it is a powerful reminder of the continuity of human existence across time and place.

By 5:00, work was halted. The four bents had been raised and connected by timbers and the basic shape of the barn stood tall in the warm afternoon sun. Yet much still needed to be done, including the hazardous fitting of the upper girts and braces, floor joists for the second floor, and a barrel of trunnels that needed to be driven home. But that was for tomorrow. Tools were packed away, the site cleaned up, and after a brief period of rest and reflection, those who had stayed the day wearily found their way to their cars and trucks, most committed to returning tomorrow to finish the job. A few of us from the board, along with George and some Foundation members, stayed a bit longer to make sure all was set for the next morning and reflect on what we had been part of. Despite our exhaustion, I still remember the glow on everyone's face; it had truly been an experience beyond our expectations. We laughed, chatted about the many moments that stood out in each of our minds; the work, those who had taken part, and hundreds who had come to watch. We had wanted an old fashioned community barn raising and we got it, it had far exceeded our most optimistic hopes. And another day awaited; but how could we top today?

Sunday morning was bright and sunny and the humidity had lifted a bit, it promised to be a beautiful day to wrap up the raising. As the parking areas began to fill again, it looked as if the day's attendance would even exceed Saturday's. Prior to work however, the Foundation had planned a special concert to help celebrate the raising of the Munger Barn; traditional fife and drum music performed by the *Stony Creek Fife and Drum Corps* and their guests *St. Mary's Fife and Drum Corps* from Limerick, Ireland. Both Corps play with those two simple instruments a style of music that dates back to the 18th century; music Captain William Dudley and many of his descendants would have found familiar. Mark Dudley, a long-time member of the *Stony Creek Corps*, had arranged for the special tribute and those in attendance that morning were not disappointed. Gathering on the deck under the still unfinished frame, the two groups played a series of rousing tunes, separately and then together. The camaraderie of the two groups was instantly evident and the growing crowd gathering at the farm was quickly swept up by their energy.

Like the Native blessing the day before, the performance only further galvanized the sense that all involved were partaking in an event that transcended time and culture, reinforcing the understanding that we are all part of something greater than ourselves, part of a community that recognizes and celebrates the uniqueness, qualities, and talents that we each bring to it. For me in retrospect, it brought to mind the words of *The Guilford Covenant* signed by the town's first settlers in 1639, so many of them David Dudley's ancestors, "...that we will, the Lord assisting us, sit down and join ourselves together ... and be helpful to one another in any common work, according to every man's ability and as need shall require..."[2] Here we were, close to 300 years later and for at least this weekend, rekindling the spirit of those words.

By 11:00 it was back to work, hoisting girts and joists, hammering in trunnels, and doing all those last details needed to secure the frame's final form. The pace quickened as those with experience guided those without through the intricacies of trimming a mortise or persuading a stubborn floor joist as men and women swarmed across the deck and up into the timbers of the frame making it into a beehive of activity. The curious kept coming, many simply pulling in to the farm as they drove by, often stunned by what they were seeing. Seasoned spectators were only too happy to share what they knew as new arrivals gawked in amazement, shielding their eyes from the sun with their hands. It was a sight to see. And through it all, the *String Band* played on.

As the afternoon drew to a close, so did the work. Thankfully by then, George had slowed down a bit, trusting his partner Gene Jones to handle much of the directing high up in the timbers. A temporary floor was thrown across some of the second story floor joists and as the work slowed and those who had been part in the raising, men and women, worker and volunteer, gathered on the deck and up in the timbers for a photo reminiscent of those often taken in the 19th century. In those old photographs, men stood or sat proudly on every part of the frame they had erected, posing in a testimony to their skill and sense of community. Now it was our turn, proud smiles and laughter, captured forever by the cameras of our day.

Prior to the gathering on the deck and frame, a small pine tree was secured to the top girt on the gable end, in one of the construction industry's oldest customs and a must for the Munger frame. Steeped in tradition, the practice, called Topping Out, symbolizes the completion of a project. It can be traced back to a Scandinavian myth that suggested that humans originated from trees and that our souls return to trees after death, thus each tree has a spirit of its own. Tradition has it that prior to cutting trees to be used to build a home, ancient Scandinavians would speak to the forest to remind it of the consideration they had always shown towards the trees and ask them to grant the use of some of them in the construction of a home. When the house was completed, the topmost leafy branch of a tree used would be set on top of the roof so that the spirits of the trees used would not become homeless – they would now dwell in the house itself. The gesture was also done to convince the tree spirits of the builder's sincere appreciation for allowing the home to be built.

Eventually the connection with tree worship changed and the individual tree spirits merged into a single forest god that passed spiritually from tree to tree. Subsequently, a tree was no longer secured to a home to appease individual tree spirits, but to ask the forest god for his blessing and protection. Thus the tree on top of the home came to symbolize the hope that his blessing would be ensured for the home, its occupants, and the land around it. Though most of us at the time might not have known it, that tree placed on the top girt, three stories up, was a powerful symbol of all our wishes for the Munger Barn's future.

At 5:00p.m. the call rang out—"work's done!" Work was halted and under the timbers of the reborn barn frame a forty foot trestle table of planks and sawhorses was quickly put together. Just as at barn raisings in the past when the frame was completed and all who had participated in some way would gather for a celebratory meal, we had planned one for those at the Dudley Farm that day. Basking under the shadow of those sturdy timbers, we feasted on a sumptuous meal brought by individuals and local businesses, much of it donated by local caterer Larry Santamaria. There is really something special about sitting down and celebrating together with food and drink alongside those you had worked so hard with to accomplish what was once simply a dream. As we sat beside that simple wooden table or mingled among those meandering about the deck, it was hard for anyone to not feel good about what the Dudley Foundation had managed to do; bring a community together around an old barn given new life.

As the celebration wore down, and people began to drift slowly to their cars, it was clear from their faces that each had made their own connection with the past. It wasn't just a look of satisfaction for a job well done, it was deeper than that. We had each made a remarkable personal connection to the past through the raising and in the process been part of something much greater than ourselves. Together we had breathed new life into that old barn and the Dudley Farm itself. The Munger Barn had begun its second life through an event that had allowed us all to renew an understanding of what the Dudley Farm is all about. Clearly it is a museum dedicated to preserving and depicting a long past time and way of life. But it was more than that and we all felt it that weekend. Those bents were raised through the sum total of all our efforts, whether it was buying a trunnel, donating food, helping to lift the timbers, or just being there. We renewed our faith in each other, the goodness of the community, and what we all could accomplish together. When William Dudley signed the Guilford Covenant aboard that immigrant ship back in 1639, this is what he and his fellow community members meant. The best of the past now lives in us all; we raised a barn.

Looking back now at that remarkable time, I have come to realize how important the raising was for the Dudley Farm. Although it would take close to two years to finish the barn, it did indeed breathe new life into the farm as an organization. It now has a multi-use facility that can be rented out for events such as weddings, is a home to permanent and temporary displays, and is a magnificent building both inside and out. First time visitors are always impressed with its soaring timbers and dramatic spaces. The building itself has become an important asset and a major attraction. But more important than the structure and its value is how the raising revitalized an organization that was beginning to lose its way and in the process of reaching out to the community restored its commitment to the very purpose of why the farm was preserved to begin with. Remembrance.

It would take another two plus years to actually complete the barn and receive from the Town of Guilford an occupancy certificate. The slow pace of the work was due to the scope of the exterior and interior work, the reliance on as much volunteer labor as possible, and limits associated with ability to finance the completion. At board meetings, the members often fell into disagreements over design, use, and whether to pay for work or rely on volunteers thus slowing progress. Through it all however, Henry Tichy oversaw the work doing much of it himself with the help of Bob Ashman, Bill Barnes, Ted Tichy, and a caste of others. Many local businesses and individuals donated services or materials to finish the ground level in particular which was turned into a heated, multi-use space. It wasn't easy, but it got done.

On August 21, 2005, almost three years to the day of the raising, the Munger Barn was officially dedicated. In Janet's words, the dedication was to "…the Dudley Foundation past, present and future, the preservation of early farm life in North Guilford, and the community of volunteers who turned our dream into the beautiful building you see today."[3] A much more sedate affair than the raising, the celebration recognized and thanked all who had contributed to the Munger Barn's completion and following a ribbon cutting ceremony at which three generations of Henry and Evelynne Tichy's family cut the ribbon, the barn was officially opened.

It was a bittersweet time for me. Following the raising I continued my role as curator at the farm, remained on the board as vice president, and tried to stay as active as I could. But as in all situations, circumstances change and life takes one in different directions, and so it was for me and the Dudley Farm. The three years following the raising saw a shift in focus for the Dudley Foundation. The loss of the education program had been a blow from which its mission never really recovered and a retrenchment of sorts took place over time. Whereas the education link had begun to propel the farm into an increasingly active regional role, one in retrospect that some board members had always been a bit leery, its end began the process of pulling back to a simpler North Guilford oriented focus. This process was gradual, but quite significant. It also went to the very heart of what had always lay beneath so many of the differences and disagreements that had divided the board of directors from the outset.

A more expansive and ambitious regional role for Dudley Farm, one typified by the education program in the end had only grudgingly been embraced by some. This brought to light the traditional suspicion of outsiders and even those from "down town". Despite the successes associated with reaching beyond the confines of North Guilford, culminating with the Munger Barn Raising, in the end there was always an issue of comfort. During the three years between the Munger Barn raising and the dedication, as it became clear that Guilford Public Schools were not interested in re-establishing a partnership with the farm and that the farm did not have the inclination or resources to pursue a program on its own, the status quo became comfortable. The Dudley Foundation turned inward.

With the barn built and rentals for weddings and family reunions beginning to become its main focus, with established events like the Farmer's Market and Farm Day, the board grew increasingly content to go with what seemed safe and worked rather than take on new and possibly risky ventures. Those battles had been fought; the Barrows Farm and the Munger Barn exemplified them. It was the risk involved with both projects along with the partnership with the schools that had substantially helped to make the farm what it was but by 2005 it was clear that the Munger Barn had brought that period of dynamic growth and energy to an end. It was time to turn back to what in many ways had typified North Guilford from its colonial beginning; an insular community built around self-reliance.

There was one new venture that began during this time that came to consume a substantial amount of the board's energy and focus; the creation of a book about the history of North Guilford. This project was quickly embraced by the members of the board, almost all North Guilford residents, and it soon became apparent that the further development of the farm as a museum or institution would not be the primary focus. A laudable and ambitious goal, for me it signaled a change of direction that made it evident that the Dudley Farm had shifted its mission. Now a local, North Guilford museum, it had become an important focal point of that community and in that aspect, it turns out many of the Foundation's members are quite happy with. I had always seen the Dudley Farm as more than that and thus it became clear it was time to move on.

Now, as the Dudley Farm begins its third decade, with an established and stable membership, its focus has remained generally local though Janet and others continue to work to expand its reach. Staid and secure, the farm has maintained an active schedule of locally oriented events and activities and of this writing; its *Voices From North Guilford* is now available. It is another crowning achievement for the Dudley Foundation and one it should be proud of.

As for me, when I decided to scale back and then end my involvement with the Dudley Farm, I had taken on new commitments that meant I could no longer devote long hours to it. But I left content in the knowledge that I had contributed to the creation of something unique and incredibly special. I had striven to help turn a surviving but run down 19th century farm into a treasure that has been preserved for generations to come. The experience was beyond my expectations and for that I will always be grateful. Through the process I had come to recognize that a small dedicated group can create something extraordinary and through a common commitment learn from one another and make a difference for others. Together we had preserved history and brought recognition of that history to a larger community. Together we had saved a farm and in the process found for us each our own redemption with the past.

Dudley Family circa 1868.
This photograph was found in the house shortly after the North Guilford
Fire Company took possession in 1992. None of the individuals are identi-
fied. Photo Courtesy of the Dudley Foundation

Raising the first bent of the Munger Barn, August 24, 2002
Photo Credit· Janet Dudley

The Dudley Farm House.
The original 1844 section is in the center, the 1860's addition to the right, and the late 19th century addition to the far left. Photo Credit: James T. Powers, 2010

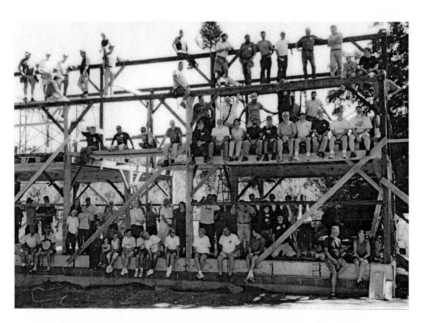

Gathering on the Munger Barn frame, August 25, 2002.
Photo Credit: Janet Dudley

Notes

Chapter One

Epigraph: Chineese proverb. Unknown authorship.

1. Steiner, B. C. (1975 (Reprint of 1897 edition)). *The History of Guilford and Madison*. Guilford: Guilford Free Library.

Interlude Number One: Powers, J. (2004, March). "A Sense of Place." *Farm News*, pp. 1-2.

Chapter Two

Epigraphy: Albert Einstein. Quote widely attributed to him; exact source unknown.

1. Kunstler, J. H. (1996, September). "Home From Nowhere." *Atlantic Monthly*. Online, pp. 1-25.

Interlude Number Two: Van Tassel, K. (July, 1999). "Dudley Farm." *Farm News*, p. 5.

Chapter Three

Epigraphy: William James. BrainyQuote.com, Xplore Inc, 2012. http://www.brainyquote.com/quotes/quotes/w/williamjam121751.html, accessed December 13, 2012.

1. *Guilford Land Records*, Volume 7, Page 66. Guilford, Connecticut: Town of Guilford, 1746.

2. *Guilford Probate Records*, Volume 8, Page 304. Guilford, Connecticut: Town of Guilford, 1761.

3. Farmland Information Center. "2007 NRI: Changes in Land Cover/Use - Agricultural Land." 2007. www.farmlandinfo.org (accessed April 17, 2012).

4. Farmland Information Center. "2007 NRI: Changes in Land Cover/Use - Agricultural Land." 2007. www.farmlandinfo.org (accessed April 17, 2012).

5. Seltzer, Curtis. "Loss of farmland: What does it mean?" LandThink. April 30, 2011. www.landthink.com (accessed April 17, 2012).

6. Civco, Daniel L., Hurd, James D., Arnold, Chester L., Prisloe, Sandy. *Characterization of Suburban Sprawl and Forest Fragmentation Through Remote Sensing Applications.* Storrs: University of Connecticut, 2000.

7. Johnston, Robert J.,Campson, Tammy Warner, Duke, Joshua M. *The Value of Farm and Forest Preservation in Connecticut.* Storrs: University of Connecticut and University of Delaware, 2007.

8. *Shoreline Times Newspaper.* "Indenture of Rebecca Dudley, 1749." 1901.

9. Gravestone Inscription: North Guilford Burial Ground, Rebecca Dudley, 1782, 1998

Interlude Number Three: Powers, James. "A Sense of Place." *Farm News,* March 2004: 1-2.

Chapter Four

Epigraphy: Frank Lloyd Wright. The quote comes from one of Wright's Two Lectures on Architecture titled "In the Realm of Ideas," delivered at the Art Institute of Chicago in 1931.

1. Gravestone Inscription: Luther Dudley, North Guilford Burial Ground, 1810, 1998

2. Gravestone Inscription: Luther Dudley, North Guilford Burial Ground, 1799, 1998

Interlude Number Four: Van Tassel, Katrina. "The Long View." *Farm News,* March 2000.

Chapter Five

Epigraphy: Yeats, William Butler "He Wishes for the Cloths of Heaven." *The Wind Among the Reeds,* Volume 3, 1899.

1. *Guilford Probate Records,* Volume 17, Pages 257-258. Guilford, Connecticut: Town of Guilford, 1811.

2. *Guilford Probate Records,* Volume 17, Pages 269-70. Guilford, Connecticut: Town of Guilford, 1811.

3. *Guilford Land Records,* Volume 21, Page 199. Guilford, Connecticut: Town of Guilford, 1811.

4. *Guilford Land Records*, Volume 22, Page 48. Guilford, Connecticut: Town of Guilford, 1812.

Interlude Number Five: Powers, James. "Curator's Corner." *Farm News*, March 2001: 3-4.

Chapter Six

Epigraph: Mark Twain. Quote widely attributed to him; exact source unknown.

1. Effgen, Alex. Hunt, Jonathan. Johnson, Bryan. Leake, Jon. "Our First Day at the Dudley Farm." *Farm News*, December 1994.
2. Evans, Oliver. *The Young Mill-Wright and Miller's Guide*. 1795 (Reprint 1989), Ayer, Salem, New Hampshire.
3. Smith, James, interview by James Powers and Leddy, Thomas. *Why the Dudley Farm is Important* (Essay) (1994).

Interlude Number Six: Smith, James, interview by James Powers and Leddy, Thomas. *Why the Dudley Farm is Important* (Essay) (1994).

Chapter Seven

Epigraph: Beecher, Henry Ward. *Seven Lectures to a Young Man*, 1844. (A pamphlet).

1. "Harriet Beecher Stowe Family." *The Harriet Beecher Stowe Center*. 2011. www.harrietbeecherstowecenter.org/hbs/beecher_family (accessed September 23, 2011).
2. Steiner, Bernard Christian. *The History of Guilford and Madison*. Guilford: Guilford Free Library, 1975 (Reprint of 1897 edition).
3. Smith, Ralph D. *The History of Guilford, Connecticut*. Bowie, Maryland: Heritage, 1990 (Reprint of 1887 edition): 34.
4. *Guilford Land Records*, Volume 21, Page 199. Guilford, Connecticut: Town of Guilford, 1811.
5. *Guilford Land Records*, Volume 32, Page 284. Guilford, Connecticut: Town of Guilford, 1841.
6. *Guilford Land Records*, Volume 36, Page 90. Guilford, Connecticut: Town of Guilford, 1841.

7. Powers, James. *The Dudley Tannery Site Survey* (March 19, 2011).

8. *Guilford Land Records*, Volume 36, Page 90. Guilford, Connecticut: Town of Guilford, 1841.

Interlude Number Seven: Powers, James. "Surviving the Drought." *Farm News*, October 1999: 1-2.

Chapter Eight

Epigraph: David Frost. BrainyQuote.com, Xplore Inc, 2012. http://www.brainyquote.com/quotes/quotes/d/davidfrost107983.html, accessed December 13, 2012.

Interlude Eight: Powers, James. "Maple Sugaring." *Farm News*, March 2000: 1-2.

Chapter Nine

Epigraph: Tolle, Eckhart. *The Power of Now*. New World Library. 1997

1. Dudley, Sophia Rossiter. "The Diary of Sophia Rossiter Dudley." Connecticut: The Guilford Free Library, 1940.

2. Dudley, Erastsus. *Erastus Dudley Ledger*. Guilford, Connecticut: Guilford Free Library, n.d.

3. *Guilford Land Records*, Volume 40, Page 177. Guilford, Connecticut: Town of Guilford, 1864.

Interlude Nine: Van Tassel, Katrina. "Pruning." *Farm News*, July 1999.

Chapter Ten

Epigraph: Shinn, Florence Scovel. *The Complete Works of Florence Scovel Shinn*. Dover Edition. 2010: 13.

1. United States Census. United States Census Bureau, 1820, 1830, 1840, 1850, 1860.

2. *Guilford Land Records*, Volume 40, Page 177. Guilford, Connecticut: Town of Guilford, 1864.

3. *Guilford Probate Records*, Volume 33, Page 42. Guilford, Connecticut: Town of Guilford, 1872.

4. *Guilford Probate Records*, Volume 33, Page 42. Guilford, Connecticut: Town of Guilford, 1872.

Interlude Ten: Powers, James. "Curator's Corner." *Farm News*, March 2004: 3-4.

Chapter Eleven

Epigraph: Henry Ward Beecher. BrainyQuote.com, Xplore Inc, 2012. http://www.brainyquote.com/quotes/quotes/h/henry wardb163037.html, accessed December 13, 2012.

1. Rossiter, Morris. "Mabel Dudley Rossiter." Farm News, October 2000: 4.
2. Rossiter, Morris. "Remembrances of the Dudley Farm." *Farm News*, February 2005: 6.
3. Dudley, Nathan. "On a Day's Farming." *Farm News*, July 2000: 4-5.
4. Landgraf, Walter. "Charcoal Hearth Model Steps in Building the Pile, Rockland "Open Charcoal Pits"." *Rockland Preserve*. 2011. www.madisonct.org/rockland (accessed July 26, 2011).
5. *Guilford Probate Records*, Volume 47, Page 574 Guilford, Connecticut: Town of Guilford, 1912.
6. *Guilford Land Records*, Volume 55, Page 496. Guilford, Connecticut: Town of Guilford, 1919.
7. *Guilford Land Records*, Volume 55, Page 496 Guilford, Connecticut: Town of Guilford, 1919.
8. Teacher Testimonials, interview by Thomas Leddy and James Powers. Back to the Future Program (2001).

Interlude Number Eleven: Teacher Testimonials, interview by Thomas Leddy and James Powers. Back to the Future Program (2001).

Chapter Twelve

Epigraph: Eleanor Roosevelt. BrainyQuote.com, Xplore Inc, 2012. http://www.brainyquote.com/quotes/quotes/e/eleanorroo100940.html, accessed December 13, 2012.

1. Powers, James. "The Barn." *Farm News*, July 2002: 1-2.
2. Senerchia, George. "The Story of a Late 19th Century Barn." *Farm News*, June 2002: 4-5.

3. Powers, James "So What's a Trunnel?" *Farm News*, June 2002: 6-7.

4. Powers, James. "So What's a Trunnel?" *Farm News*, June 2002: 6-7.

Interlude Number Twelve: Jackson, Sam. "Old Barns and Men." *Old Barns and Men*. 1996. wacobelle.org/samjacksonoldbarnsandmen (accessed October 13, 2011).

Chapter Thirteen

Epigraph: Richard von Weizsaecker. BrainyQuote.com, Xplore Inc, 2012. http://www.brainyquote.com/quotes/quotes/r/richardvon112680. html, accessed December 13, 2012.

1 Powers, James. "The Raising." *Farm News*, October 2002: 2-3.

2 Steiner, Bernard Christian. *The History of Guilford and Madison.* Guilford: Guilford Free Library, 1975 (Reprint of 1897 edition).

3 Dudley, Janet, interview by James Powers. President of the Dudley Foundation (August 21, 2005)

Bibliography

1799 *United States Census. Luther Dudley.* United States Census Bureau, 1799.

1820 *United States Cesus: Erastus Dudley.* United States Census Bureau, 1820.

1830 *United States Census: Erastus Dudley.* United States Census Bureau, 1830.

1840 *United States Census: Erastus Dudley.* United States Census Bureau, 1840.

1850 *United States Census: Erastus Dudley.* United States Census Bureau, 1850.

1852 and 1856 *Maps of Guilford.* Guilford Free Library, Guilford, Connecticut.

1860 *United States Census: Erastus Dudley.* United States Census Bureau, 1860.

1870 *United States Census: Erastus Dudley.* United States Census Bureau, 1870.

Book of Terryers. Guilford, Ct: Guilford Town Records, circa 1650.

Beecher, Henry Ward. *Seven Lectures to a Young Man,* 1844. (A pamphlet).

_____. BrainyQuote.com, Xplore Inc, 2012. http://www.brainyquote.com/quotes/quotes/h/henrywardb163037.html, accessed December 13, 2012.

Civco, Daniel L., Hurd, James D., Arnold, Chester L., Prisloe, Sandy. *Characterization of Suburban Sprawl and Forest Fragmentation Through Remote Sensing Applications.* Storrs: University of Connecticut, 2000.

Diderot, Denis. *Oictoral Encyclopedia of Trades and Industry,* Volume Two (Reprint). New York: Dover, 1993.

Dudley, Albert. "The Ancestry of David Dudley." Nashua, New Hampshire, 1995.

Dudley, Erastsus. *Erastus Dudley Ledger.* Guilford, Connecticut: Guilford Free Library, n.d.

Dudley, Janet, interview by James Powers. President of the Dudley Foundation (August 21, 2005).

Dudley, Nathan. "On a Day's Farming." *Farm News*, July 2000.

Dudley, Sophia Rossiter. "The Diary of Sophia Rossiter Dudley." Connecticut: The Guilford Free Library, 1940.

Effgen, Alex. Hunt, Jonathan. Johnson, Bryan. Leake, Jon. "Our First Day at the Dudley Farm." *Farm News*, December 1994.

Evans, Oliver. *The Young Mill-Wright and Miller's Guide*. 1795 (Reprint 1989, Ayer, Salem, New Hampshire.

Farmland Information Center. "2007 NRI: Changes in Land Cover/Use - Agricultural Land." 2007. www.farmlandinfo.org (accessed April 17, 2012).

Frost, David. BrainyQuote.com, Xplore Inc, 2012. http://www.brainyquote.com/quotes/quotes/d/davidfrost107983.html, accessed December 13, 2012.

Interview by James Powers. Gravestone Inscription: Luther Dudley, North Guilford Burial Ground, 1799 (1998).

Interview by James Powers. Gravestone Inscription: Luther Dudley, North Guilford Burial Ground, 1810 (1998).

Interview by James Powers. Gravestone Inscription: Rebecca Dudley, North Guilford Burial Ground (1998).

James, William. BrainyQuote.com, Xplore Inc, 2012. http://www.brainyquote.com/quotes/quotes/w/williamjam121751.html, accessed December 13, 2012.

Guilford Land Records, Volume 21, Page 199. Guilford, Connecticut: Town of Guilford, 1811.

Guilford Land Records, Volume 22, Page 48. Guilford, Connecticut: Town of Guilford, 1812.

Guilford Land Records, Volume 32, Page 284. Guilford, Connecticut: Town of Guilford, 1841.

Guilford Land Records, Volume 36, Page 90. Guilford, Connecticut: Town of Guilford, 1841.

Guilford Land Records, Volume 40, Page 177. Guilford, Connecticut: Town of Guilford, 1864.

Guilford Land Records, Volume 7, Page 66. Guilford, Connecticut: Town of Guilford, 1746.

Guilford Land Records, Volume 55, Page 496 Guilford, Connecticut: Town of Guilford, 1919.

Guilford Probate Records, Volume 47, Page 574 Guilford, Connecticut: Town of Guilford, 1912.

Guilford Probate Records, Volume 17, Pages 257-258. Guilford, Connecticut: Town of Guilford, 1811.

Guilford Probate Records, Volume 17, Pages 269-70. Guilford, Connecticut: Town of Guilford, 1811.

_____, Volume 33, Page 42. Guilford, Connecticut: Town of Guilford, 1872.

_____, Volume 8, Page 304. Guilford, Connecticut: Town of Guilford, 1761.

"Harriet Beecher Stowe Family." *The Harriet Beecher Stowe Center*. 2011.www.harrietbeecherstowecenter.org/hbs/beecher_family (accessed September 23, 2011).

Jackson, Sam. "Old Barns and Men." *Old Barns and Men*. 1996. wacobelle.org/samjacksonoldbarnsandmen (accessed October 13, 2011).

Johnston, Robert J.,Campson, Tammy Warner, Duke, Joshua M. *The Value of Farm and Forest Preservation in Connecticut*. Storrs: University of Connecticut and University of Delaware, 2007.

Kunstler, James Howard. "Home From Nowhere." *The Atlantic Online*, September 1996: 1-25.

Landgraf, Walter. "Charcoal Hearth Model Steps in Building the Pile, Rockland "Open Charcoal Pits". *Rockland Preserve*. 2011. www.madisonct.org/rockland (accessed July 26, 2011).

Mansfield, Howard. "The Same Ax, Twice." *Yankee Magazine*, April 2000.

Powers, James. "Curator's Corner." *Farm News* , March 2000.

_____. "A Sense of Place." *Farm News*, March 2004.

_____. "Curator's Corner." *Farm News*, March 2001.

_____."Curator's Corner." *Farm News*, March 2004.

_____."Curator's Corner." *Farm News*, June 2002.

_____."Maple Sugaring." *Farm News*, March 2000.

_____."Mud." *Farm News*, March 2004: 2-3.

_____."So What's a Trunnel?" *Farm News*, June 2002.

_____."Surviving the Drought." *Farm News*, October 1999.

_____."The Barn." *Farm News*, July 2002.

_____."The Munger Barn." *Farm News*, June 2002.

_____."The Raising." *Farm News*, October 2002.

_____. *The Dudley Tannery Site Survey* (March 19, 2011).

Roosevelt, Eleanor. BrainyQuote.com, Xplore Inc, 2012. http://
www.brainyquote.com/quotes/quotes/e/eleanorroo100940.html,
accessed December 13, 2012.

Rossiter, Morris. *Farm News*, December 2005.

_____."Mabel Dudley Rossiter." *Farm News*, October 2000: 4.

_____."Remembrances of the Dudley Farm." *Farm News*,
February 2005: 6.

Seltzer, Curtis."Loss of farmland: What does it mean?" *LandThink*.
April 30, 2011. www.landthink.com (accessed April 17, 2012).

Senerchia, George."The Story of a Late 19th Century Barn." *Farm
News*, June 2002: 4-5.

Shinn, Florence Scovel. *The Complete Works of Florence Scovel Shinn.*
Dover Edition. 2010: 13.

Shoreline Times Newspaper."Indenture of Rebecca Dudley, 1749." 1901.

Smith, James, interview by James Powers and Leddy, Thomas. *Why the
Dudley Farm is Important* (Essay) (1994).

Smith, Ralph D. *The History of Guilford, Connecticut.* Bowie, Maryland:
Heritage, 1990 (Reprint of 1887 edition).

Steiner, Bernard Christian. *The History of Guilford and Madison.*
Guilford: Guilford Free Library, 1975 (Reprint of 1897 edition).

Teacher Testimonials, interview by Thomas Leddy and James Powers.
Back to the Future Program (2001).

The History of the Dudley Family. Guilford: The Guilford Free
Library, n.d.

United States Census. United States Census Bureau, 1820, 1830, 1840, 1850, 1860.

Van Tassel, Katrina. "Dudley Farm Summer." *Farm News*, March 2000

_____. "Pruning." *Farm News*, July 1999.

_____. "The Long View." *Farm News*, March 2000.

von Weizsaecker, Richard. BrainyQuote.com, Xplore Inc, 2012. http://www.brainyquote.com/quotes/quotes/r/richardvon112680.html, accessed December 13, 2012.

Yeats, William Butler "He Wishes for the Cloths of Heaven." *The Wind Among the Reeds*, Volume 3, 1899.

About the Author

JAMES T. POWERS first developed a life-long love of history while growing up in the old industrial town of Wallingford, Connecticut. Following graduation from Wesleyan University, James committed himself to a career of sharing that love through the teaching of history. Over the years, his interests and expertise have expanded to include local archaeology and the study of New England Colonial architecture both which he teaches at Guilford High School in Guilford, Connecticut. Besides a BA, James has also received two Masters Degrees from Wesleyan University. James and his wife Rita live in an 18th Century home in Durham, Connecticut that they are currently restoring and on Prince Edward Island, Canada.

HOMEBOUND
PUBLICATIONS
Independent Publisher of Contemplative Literature

AT HOMEBOUND PUBLICATIONS WE RECOGNIZE THE IMPORTANCE of going home to gather from the stores of old wisdom to help nourish our lives in this modern era. We choose to lend voice to those individuals who endeavor to translate the old truths into new context and keep alive through the written word ways of life that are now endangered. Our titles introduce insights concerning mankind's present internal, social and ecological dilemmas.

It is our intention at Homebound Publications to revive contemplative storytelling. We publish full-length introspective works of: non-fiction, essay collections, epic verse, short story collections, journals, travel writing, and novels. In our fiction titles our intention is to introduce new perspectives that will directly aid mankind in the trials we face at present.

It is our belief that the stories humanity lives by give both context and perspective to our lives. Some older stories, while well-known to the generations, no longer resonate with the heart of the modern man nor do they address the present situation we face individually and as a global village. Homebound chooses titles that balance a reverence for the old sensibilities; while at the same time presenting new perspectives by which to live.

WWW.HOMEBOUNDPUBLICATIONS.COM

CPSIA information can be obtained at www.ICGtesting.com
Printed in the USA
BVOW08s1800080913

330351BV00011B/29/P